BRAIN WORKOUT

"To the dull mind nature is leaden. To the illumined mind the whole world burns and sparkles with light."

Ralph Waldo Emerson (1803–82)

Gareth Moore

BRAIN WORKOUT

Tips and Techniques
to Train your Mind

WATKINS
Sharing Wisdom Since 1893

First published 2009 under the title *Keep your Brain Fit*
This edition first published in the UK and USA 2018 by
Watkins, an imprint of Watkins Media Limited
Unit 11, Shepperton House
89-93 Shepperton Road
London N1 3DF

enquiries@watkinspublishing.com

1 3 5 7 9 10 8 6 4 2

Designed and typeset by Clare Thorpe

Printed and bound in the United Kingdom by TJ International

A CIP record for this book is available from the British Library

ISBN: 978-1-78678-178-9

www.watkinspublishing.com

CONTENTS

FOR MY MUM AND DAD

INTRODUCTION

Keeping your brain fit is an essential part of a healthy life. Training your mind will not only help you get your head around facts and figures better, but will also enrich your experiences and counteract the effects of ageing. This book will help you discover just what your brain is capable of, and show you how to achieve this. It will challenge you with enjoyable mental gymnastics that demonstrate how, unlike physical training, working to achieve brain fitness is always fun!

GREY MATTER MATTERS

The great gift of the human brain is our ability to think and abstract, and work out new ways to do things. Computers can calculate a thousand prime numbers in the time it takes you to pick up your pen, but in general they can't even begin to scrape at the surface of what you can do on your own by simply sitting and thinking. In Chapter 1, we look at just how amazing the brain is.

Our brains don't just keep us alive: they embody every aspect of our conscious and unconscious thought. They learn and adapt to our changing needs without our even being aware of the fact. These adaptations can be temporary, such as correcting our vision as we move from a light to a dark room, or permanent, as when rebuilding mental faculties after a serious stroke. So keeping your brain fit and healthy is every bit as important as looking after the rest of your body.

Plenty of evidence shows that suitable brain exercises lead to increased mental fitness – faster thought processing, greater suppleness and agility of mind, and sharper responses. Our brains have enormous capacity – big enough to cope with two lifetimes, let alone one. By training spare neural pathways in different ways of thinking, we can build on existing skills and develop new ones, expanding our intellectual capability.

As we age, our brains gently start to slow down, both in reaction time and in the raw speed of our learning, but we can easily compensate for these changes: the more of life we've experienced and stored in all that spare space, the smarter we are. Expanding our mental faculties, at no matter what age, provides a buffer against decline. It also equips us to cope better with the ever-changing challenges of life, from using new technology, to multi-tasking, to perceiving the truth behind political "spin".

IT'S FUN TO STAY MENTALLY FIT

Physical fitness training involves serious effort and a need to take care to avoid injury. Keeping your brain fit is much easier! Whereas our bodies become toned and strong through repeating the same exercises, our brains thrive on novelty. Upgrading your mind is all about challenging yourself with new concepts and experiences. Anything you can do with only minimal thought will fail to stretch you.

Chapters 2, 4 and 6 are packed full of brain-challenging puzzles and exercises, which get progressively harder. The puzzles have all been created especially for this book, and tailored to help you identify and improve both your mental strengths and your weaknesses. In Chapter 3, we take a look at how you can improve a wide range of mental skills in day-to-day life.

JOINED-UP THINKING

As we will see, mental activity draws on a range of skills. For example, just listening to someone speak requires you to process the incoming sounds, recalling from memory the speech fragments and the words that include them, and perhaps observe the person's facial expression. Misheard words may need correcting, and understanding the sentence itself could require further recall and thought. You're using vision, hearing, memory, comprehension and logic, just to work out what's being said. Because of the brain's complex interconnectivity, skills or knowledge that we acquire in one area can also be applied in other areas. The quiz about the planet Pluto on page 34, for example, is primarily an exercise in comprehension, but it will engage your memory, your general knowledge and your numerical skills, too.

The way you approach any mental problem will be influenced by what you already know, and by how your brain has been trained to think (consciously and subconsciously) in the past. Vitally, this cross-fertilization also works in reverse: what you gain through the mental rigours of quizzes and puzzles will increase your logic, memory, observation and other skills required for learning and problem-solving. Practical hints and tips are spread throughout the book, but in Chapter 5 we look at how you can bring together a range of skills in order to solve tricky problems – both puzzles and real-world challenges.

THE PATH TO A WELL-TONED MIND

Improving your mental fitness does not need to involve a lot of time. Even just a few minutes a day can make a huge difference – depending, of course, on how much exercise your brain normally receives in your typical daily routine. Improvements are quantifiable and have been shown to last for 10 or more years, and there is abundant evidence that the more you train, the better your brain.

Whenever you can, set aside five minutes or so every day to do some of the exercises in this book. And however busy you are, follow the ideas for challenging your brain in the course of your regular routine, so that you integrate mind-stretching into your normal activities with minimal effort.

"It is not knowledge, but the act of learning, not possession but the act of getting there, which grants the greatest enjoyment."

Carl Friedrich Gauss (1777–1855)

This book will set you on the path to a well-toned mind, but that should be just the beginning. More than anything, what you can learn here is that the very act of challenging your brain will help it grow and expand its capabilities, in often unexpected ways. Enjoy the puzzles, follow the hints and tips on applying your brain training in practical ways, but, most of all, use what you've learned as a springboard for devising your own mental challenges and enriching your unique understanding of the world.

1
THE BRAIN AT WORK

Each of us possesses one of the most complex and remarkable pieces of equipment in the known universe – a human brain. This chapter outlines how the brain functions and reveals the origin of our astonishing mental capabilities.

The chapter begins with a look at the structure of the brain, and at the intricate network of connections that makes complex thought possible. Next come tips on keeping the brain healthy and improving mental fitness. The chapter also includes a look at two skills that are fundamental to both problem-solving and negotiating daily life – memory and multi-tasking.

MEET YOUR BRAIN

There was once a fear that computers might outstrip human thinking. Yet the more science reveals about the brain's functions, the more we discover about our amazing natural capacities and see we have little to fear.

THE SPEED AND POWER OF YOUR BRAIN

Your mobile phone can process around 25 billion instructions per second. This may sound a lot, but best estimates put our own processing capacity at around 100 trillion instructions per second – far more powerful.

Unlike machines, however, we can't focus all of our processing power on a single task – we need to keep breathing, stay balanced, keep listening and seeing, and so on, all at the same time. This means we're stuck with relatively slow arithmetic, an inability to remember everything we might want to, and a whole gamut of sometimes unwanted distractions, such as our emotions.

Nevertheless, we can learn to take better advantage of the processing power our brain does make available to us. One way to understand this capability is to take a look at what's inside your head, to help you realize just how remarkable your brain is.

NEURONS, SYNAPSES AND GIANT SEA SLUGS

The brain comprises two main types of cell: nerve cells, or neurons, which carry information, and a much larger number of glial cells, which perform key support functions. Neurons receive all the sensory information from our body – not just sight, smell, touch, hearing and taste, but also balance, pain, motion, temperature, and much more. Each neuron communicates with thousands of others, in a complicated web of connections that makes us capable of everything from breathing to conscious thought.

Until the mid-20th century, scientists assumed that we must have super-powered brain cells compared to those of lesser creatures, but they were wrong. In fact, there is very little difference between the way a sea slug's brain cells work and the way those in your own head function. The similarities are so great that studies on sea slugs have taught us a lot about how our own brains work. We now know that it's principally the *quantity* of brain cells that differentiates us from other, simpler animals – every human has as many brain cells as 10 million sea slugs. Before birth we grow neurons at a staggering rate of up to 250,000 per minute. Some are discarded along the way, but an adult brain still retains around 100 billion neurons.

The bridging point where one neuron connects to another is called a synapse. These connections are continually changing as we learn, modifying themselves to embed new knowledge, memories and skills in our brains. It is this malleability on a massive scale that makes our brains superior to those of any other creatures, allowing us to think, feel, reason and deduce, and defining precisely who we are. Connections that aren't used may be removed – in the two years after puberty, our brains are spring-cleaned and we lose an average of 5,000 synapses every second. Nevertheless, this still results in an adult brain of around 500 trillion synapses. Such an enormous figure gives just one indication of the astonishing flexibility of our brains: remember that every one of these synapses can be modified in order to let you learn something new.

THE CEREBRAL CORTEX

More than two-thirds of the weight of a human brain is accounted for by the outer layer, the cerebral cortex. This layer gives rise to our higher levels of conscious awareness, reasoning, communication skills and creativity. Beneath it are the cerebellum and other structures that evolved earlier and so provide more primitive responses, such as immediate reactions to perceived threats.

These reactions not only pre-empt our conscious responses but, sometimes critically for survival, are much faster, too. Unfortunately, they are not always useful today – freezing when you see a car coming toward you is not a helpful response.

The cerebral cortex is divided into two hemispheres that are joined through a large number of synaptic connections. In general, the left side deals with specifics and the right side with broader concepts. However, the popular belief that people are mainly either left- or

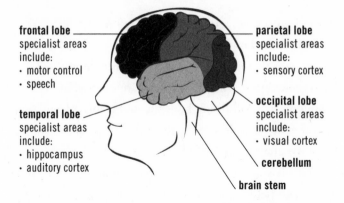

frontal lobe
specialist areas
include:
· motor control
· speech

temporal lobe
specialist areas
include:
· hippocampus
· auditory cortex

parietal lobe
specialist areas
include:
· sensory cortex

occipital lobe
specialist areas
include:
· visual cortex

cerebellum

brain stem

right-brained, and that this produces different thinking styles, is too simplistic. In fact, the two hemispheres tend to act in concert, and we use both sides of our brain all the time. For this reason, you'll get the greatest benefit from practising a wide range of mental activities in order to exercise as much of your brain as possible. Even highly specific puzzles, such as those to test numerical ability, will draw on more than just that particular type of thinking skill.

REGIONS OF THE BRAIN

The cerebral cortex is further subdivided into regions called lobes, as shown above. Each lobe contains certain key skill centres dedicated to particular tasks – but these skills are specific. So it's not the case that, for example, all visual thought occurs in the occipital lobe, where the visual cortex is located. This area performs initial processing of the information received by our eyes, but this doesn't mean that when we think consciously about shapes we are only using this one region. Similarly, although the hippocampus is strongly associated with long-term memory, more memory is also distributed across the brain. Most importantly, our conscious thought is spread throughout the brain, and information from many areas has to be integrated in order to give rise to a specific thought or action.

This is a key reason why improving one aspect of your brain can help others. Because everything in your head is so massively interconnected, laying down new thinking pathways lets your thoughts travel faster, more direct routes not just for one skill but for them all.

MAINTAIN YOUR BRAIN

Our brains are fearsome consumers. We can help keep them fit by ensuring that we provide them with the raw materials and ideal conditions they need for their proper function.

A POWER-HUNGRY MACHINE

Despite making up only 2 per cent of our body weight, our brains use around 20 per cent of all the energy we consume. The brain needs a steady supply of oxygen and many other chemicals in order to function, and deficits can lead to a wide range of problems, from minor fatigue through to serious brain damage. Each neuron has a very limited store of energy, so when working at high speed it needs a rapid supply of more oxygen and nutrients from the blood. Physical fitness helps to improve blood circulation; therefore, it's an important aspect of your ability to do almost any mental activity. Studies have shown that improvements in physical fitness can lead to corresponding gains in mental performance.

THE EFFECT OF DIET

When we eat, our digestive system breaks down food into chemicals that enter our bloodstream and are carried to our brain. It's been suggested that certain substances, such as omega-3 fatty acids (found in foods such as oily fish), promote good brain function. More generally, a varied diet, containing a wide range of foods, is essential not for good physical and mental health.

CHEMICALS AND THE BRAIN

Most of the chemicals in our blood are prevented from entering the brain by a special gateway known as the blood–brain barrier. However, in addition to essentials such as oxygen, certain molecules that encode messages to and from the brain are allowed to pass through. Many drugs, such as medicines, recreational drugs, and even alcohol and caffeine, work by utilizing the brain's communication system in this way. Medicines must be used with care, while recreational drugs should be avoided altogether. Certain drugs trick the brain's pleasure circuitry to "reward" you with artificial highs of happiness. If the drugs are taken too often, the brain learns to expect these chemicals, and reacts to any lack of them as a problem, producing unpleasant and sometimes severe withdrawal symptoms.

STRESS – STIMULATING OR DEBILITATING?

Stress is a biological call to attention. In small amounts, it can aid concentration and give you the motivation to complete a task. However, an over-stressed mind does not learn nearly as efficiently as a calm mind does. Long-term stress places your body in a continually heightened state, ready to react to threats. Over time, this can lead to an increased susceptibility to illness, weight gain, or more serious health complications.

Tackling stress involves identifying the source, such as an unpleasant working environment, then changing or removing whatever is causing the problem – even if this seems difficult in the short term. More minor stress can often be alleviated by physical exercise, social interaction, laughter and sleep.

THE BRAIN'S MEMORY BANKS

You've probably heard of people who can perform amazing feats of memory – recalling hundreds of digits in sequence, for example. In fact, there is little difference in raw ability between these people and you. We can all improve our memory with practice and by using simple tactics.

SHORT- AND LONG-TERM MEMORY

Memory can be split at its most basic level into short-term and long-term, or things we remember for up to a few minutes and things we can recall much later. The fact that we forget most of the information that we take in is a critical part of our ability to function normally – our brains discard information they think we don't need in order to prevent our minds from being overwhelmed with lots of useless information.

Despite this, we retain more information than we realize, but don't have a way to activate many of these memories unless they are triggered by some other thought. Even then, locked-away long-term memories are often unconsciously mixed with newer memories when they are finally recalled, so should not be relied upon.

Long-term memory is not just about explicit storing of facts. It also includes procedural memory. Generally, this concerns difficult skills that, once acquired, we never forget, such as how to balance on a bicycle. These memories are defined as implicit because, despite your being able to act on them, they are generally very hard to recall consciously – try explaining how to ride a bicycle, for example.

WORKING MEMORY

Part of our short-term memory is called working memory. This can typically store between four and nine pieces of information, which we must continually rehearse if we wish not to forget them – the digits of a phone number are a good example. Without working memory, you'd be unable to read this sentence because you'd have forgotten the beginning by the time you reached the end, and your brain wouldn't be able to decode the meaning.

Memory is therefore crucial in all aspects of life. Given this critical nature, perhaps your memory isn't as bad as you think – if it works fine for implicit things (see p.25), you can learn to use it better for explicit things such as making shopping lists in your head and remembering names.

The good news is that suitable memory training has been shown to lead to significant improvements that last for many years. Each of the exercise chapters in this book includes a section of memory tests, which are designed to help you extend your memory.

MEMORY AND EMOTIONS

We remember vivid details of key moments in our lives, such as the moment we got our exam results or what we were doing the day we heard about a major disaster. The circumstantial details are unimportant to remember but our brains don't know that – we had extreme emotions at the time and so even trivial details were stored as if of critical importance.

If you want to remember something, therefore, associating it with a strong emotion will make the task much easier. Another good way is to link people or facts to ridiculous images that make you laugh.

THE MULTI-TASKING MIND

Our brains can do an incredible number of things at once. Despite this amazing multi-tasking ability, we can only consciously think a single thought at any one time.

UNCONSCIOUS PROCESSES

Even when we're not consciously thinking, our brains are performing a huge variety of simultaneous operations. These happen automatically – which is lucky, because otherwise we might forget to breathe! We are born with many processing capacities, such as the dedicated circuits that interpret visual information as lines and shapes, while others are learned as we grow. Many of these circuits are layered one on top of another – for example, we may identify certain shapes as facial features, and then further processing converts these into names and memories of people we recognize, all without conscious effort.

Much of this processing is vital to help us make sense of the world: without it, we'd be swamped by information. However, on rare occasions when it goes wrong, we can't disable it, even when we know we're mistaken.

We see the moon's craters or the windows and doors of houses as "faces", and we're taken in by optical illusions, because of the huge amount of unconscious processing in our visual system.

CONSCIOUS THOUGHTS

Different sets of neurons learn different skills. As a result, we can cope consciously with several stimuli at once – so long as these are completely different, such as visual images and sound. It's only when we try to process two similar stimuli – for example, trying to listen to two separate conversations at the same time – that we

THINKING STRAIGHT

In any mental task or challenge, promoting concentration and focus will enable you to use your brain to its maximum capability.

- Choose a tidy, quiet environment with minimal distractions. Close the door, take the phone off the hook, and shut down your e-mail.
- Commit mentally to the length of a task or work session, and promise yourself not to get distracted in that time period.
- Take time to plan what to do, so you focus on the most appropriate parts of the task. You'll then work faster, with fewer mistakes.
- Try to focus on a single task at once. Juggling two tasks may overtax your working memory and cause you to lose track of both.
- If you do need to switch focus to another task, then try to move cleanly between the two so that thoughts from the previous task do not keep interrupting the new task. Make a rapid "brain dump" by jotting your thoughts down on paper, noting what you were working on and anything you wish to remember for when you return later.
- Set yourself achievable goals so that you have a structure for timing and rewarding yourself. Remember to include time for breaks. Set yourself deadlines if you know they help you to focus.

lose our train of thought. This helps explain why many of us are happy to listen to music while simultaneously reading or writing, but get distracted when we try to listen to the lyrics as well. We also rapidly become conditioned to ignore background music – we "tune it out" – so long as it stays at a reasonably constant volume.

2
START-UP
EXERCISES

The nerve networks in our brains are densely interconnected – and for this reason, improving our mental powers involves working on a wide variety of skills. To help you keep track of your progress in a range of areas, the exercises in this book are broken down into verbal, visual and spatial, numerical, logical reasoning, and memory tasks.

The puzzles in this chapter provide a gentle warm-up in each of these areas. You may well find that you're stronger or more confident in some areas than in others, but to gain the greatest benefit, make sure that you work through all of them. Full solutions are given at the end of the chapter. The point of these exercises is not to give you a "pass" or "fail" mark, but to build on your strengths and increase your understanding across the full breadth of mental skills – and perhaps even expose you to types of thinking you rarely engage in.

MAKING A START

This is the first of three chapters of tasks designed to work on all aspects of your mental skills. For a good brain workout, try to complete all of the sections. You can do them anywhere, as long as you won't be disturbed.

HINTS AND TIPS

Inevitably, you'll find some puzzles easier than others, so challenge yourself to do those quickly. If you find a puzzle hard and don't know how to solve it, see if you can find the method by experimenting – this can be a great brain workout in itself. If you're still stuck, turn to the solution, then have another go at that puzzle tomorrow. This "reverse engineering" approach is perfectly acceptable, as it extends your understanding.

When attempting the visual tasks, try to solve them without using any aids, such as rotating the book, using a mirror, or labelling the picture. Similarly for the numeric and verbal tasks, the more you can calculate without writing notes, the better. Most of the logic and reasoning puzzles can be solved in your head, but you may find making notes helpful. For memory tasks, writing notes at all is cheating and will nullify the point of the challenge.

Remember, the aim is not necessarily to solve each puzzle but simply to try – the process of making your brain work in these areas matters more than the final result. Don't spend too long on any one puzzle – generally, 10 minutes per page should be enough.

VERBAL TASKS 1

The following puzzles target various aspects of your verbal skills. These include your vocabulary, ability to spot alternative meanings of words, skill in identifying words from jumbled letters, and ability to retain details.

LETTER CHOICE *(solutions on page 50)*

Delete one letter from each of the following letter pairs in order to reveal a different word on each line.

1 EH AI XS RY
2 ST TR IR EA LT
3 ST EO LM OU ST IR NO NG
4 TU RN ID CE RK SY TO RA DN SD
5 DC LE ON BI RA SL
6 VT EA MN IE TR YI ET DY
7 HC HE LI VI CA LO PR YT AE DR
8 DE XE AU LO TR ES SD

MIXED-UP SENTENCES *(solutions on page 51)*

Find an anagram of the CAPITALIZED word to complete each sentence.

1 The diver went down to the DEEPS at top ___
2 The SENATOR was arrested for committing ___
3 He needed a PLASTER after an accident with the ___
4 The stolen GADGET had been security-___
5 She ran and hid AMONG the ___ trees

6 The landlord vowed to be ___ with future RENTERS

7 After ORIENTATING herself, she began the ___

8 It was difficult to ___ without SHATTERING it

SYNONYM SETS *(solutions on page 51)*

Draw lines to link each word in the grid with one other word that can have a similar meaning. All words should be used once and once only.

joining	entrancing	tending	approaching
pending	tearing	promising	developing
combining	proposing	growing	enduring
captivating	caring	suffering	ripping

COMPREHENSION *(solutions on page 51)*

Read the following passages, then try to answer the questions below them without checking back. Repeat until you've answered them all.

> Pluto was reclassified in 2006 as a dwarf planet. The solar system now has only 8 full planets. Pluto, discovered in 1930 by Clyde Tombaugh, who was 24, was excluded because it had not "swept clean" its area of space.

1 What type of planet was Pluto reclassified as?

2 How old was Tombaugh when he discovered Pluto?

3 Why was Pluto reclassified?

A rainbow is an example of "chromatic dispersion". When white light hits a drop of water in the atmosphere, some of the light is refracted into the drop itself. This splits the light into its component colours. Some light is then reflected inside the drop and is refracted back out, splitting even more strongly into its component colours.

4 What two-word term is a rainbow described as "an example of"?

5 After splitting into its component colours, what first happens to some of the light before it leaves the water drop again?

6 What happens twice to create such strong component colours?

CRYPTOGRAM *(solution on page 51)*

By replacing each letter in the following with the one immediately after it in the alphabet, how quickly can you decode this quotation?

Hs hr mdudq snn kzsd sn ad vgzs xnt lhfgs gzud addm

Fdnqfd Dkhns

ODD-ONE-OUT ROUND 1 *(solutions on page 52)*

Using your general knowledge, can you work out which is the odd one out in each of the following sets of words?

Sonnet	Mean	Sea
Ballad	Meter	Castle
Limerick	Mode	Paper
Prose	Midrange	Bag
Ode	Median	Stone

VISUAL AND SPATIAL TASKS 1

These workouts test your ability to visualize and manipulate objects in your head. The following puzzles cover not only simple transformations such as rotation and reflection, but also more complex changes such as 3D folding and geometric progression. In each case, look for identifiable parts of the image that can be used as visual hooks to help you keep track of the problem you're solving.

VISUAL SEQUENCES (solutions on page 52)

Identify which option, A, B or C, completes each series of three figures.

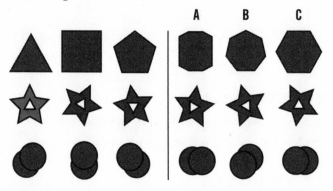

REFLECTION *(solution on page 52)*

Try to copy the pattern below on to the empty grid beside it so that the image is reflected in the vertical "mirror line" down the middle.

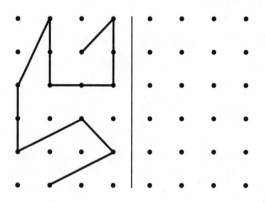

ROTATION *(solution on page 52)*

Now try copying the pattern below, but this time rotate it clockwise through a quarter of a revolution (90°), as shown by the arrow.

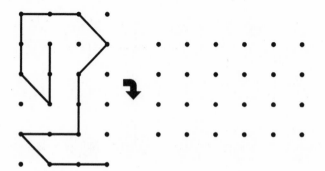

SHAPE FOLDING *(solution on page 53)*

Imagine what this "shape net" would look like if it were cut out and then folded up to make a 3D pyramid. Which one of the three following pyramids would result from this process?

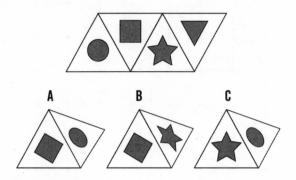

A   **B**   **C**

SHAPE COUNTING *(solution on page 53)*

Look at this abstract figure and see how many triangles of all shapes and sizes you can count. There are quite a few!

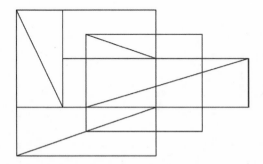

FEATURE SPOTTING *(solutions on page 53)*

Study the picture and then see how quickly you can spot where each of the following zoomed-in (but not rotated) extracts comes from.

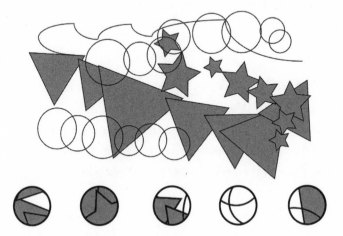

IN YOUR HEAD *(solutions on page 53)*

So far you've encountered various different visual transformations – so now here are some puzzles in which you have to create the entire image inside your head before you can solve them.

- How many straight edges are there on a cube?
- If you hold a cube in your hand, what is the maximum number of corners visible at any one time?
- What is the minimum number of triangles you can place side by side in order to make a regular (equal-sided) pentagon?

NUMERICAL TASKS 1

It's time to work on your arithmetical and number skills. It doesn't matter if you think you're good at maths or bad – none of the following exercises require any particularly difficult calculations. Each can be tackled by being mentally organized and working out the result step by step.

NUMBER SEQUENCES *(solutions on page 53)*

Each of the following sequences uses a simple mathematical rule to progress from one number to the next. By working out what these rules are, can you write in the next number in the following cases?

1	2	4	8	16	___
3	5	8	12	17	___
11	16	21	26	31	___
1	3	9	27	81	___
123	111	99	87	75	___

NUMERICAL THINKING *(solutions on page 54)*

By thinking mathematically, can you answer each of the following questions?

- If I buy a pack of 12 eggs, but accidentally break 25 per cent of them on the way home, and then cook a third of those that remain, how many whole uncooked eggs do I have left?

- I'm planning to put up a 10-metre fence in my garden. If this requires two fence posts per metre, how many fence posts will I need in total?
- If I run at 6mph (miles per hour) for half an hour, and then walk at 4mph for another quarter of an hour, how far have I travelled?

PROBABLE PROBLEMS *(solutions on page 54)*

In each of these cases, can you work out which of the two listed events is the *most likely* to occur? For bonus marks, what are the actual mathematical probabilities of each event?

- Rolling a 3 on a 6-sided die; *or* getting heads both times when tossing a coin twice
- Rolling a total of 12 on two 6-sided dice; *or* picking the Ace of Spades or the Queen of Clubs in a random selection from a normal pack of 52 playing cards.

TIME PASSES *(solutions on page 54)*

Can you work out how many hours and minutes have elapsed between each of these pairs of times?

5:50pm	to	7:30pm	=	_____
10:30am	to	4:20pm	=	_____
6am	to	midnight	=	_____
3:45pm	to	10:25pm	=	_____
1:23am	to	2:34pm	=	_____

THIS TIME TOMORROW (solutions on page 54)

Given the time in the country on the left, what time is it in the one on the right? Use this table of world time offsets to help you work it out.

Sydney	Beijing	Moscow	London	New York	Waikiki
GMT+10	GMT+8	GMT+3	GMT	GMT−5	GMT−10

today/tomorrow/yesterday

1 1pm in Beijing   =   ___   in London   _____
2 3:30am in New York =   ___   in Waikiki   _____
3 10:20am in Waikiki   =   ___   in Beijing   _____
4 4pm in Sydney   =   ___   in New York _____
5 11pm in Moscow   =   ___   in Sydney   _____
6 Midnight in London =   ___   in Beijing   _____

A-MAZING NUMBERS (solutions on page 55)

By moving horizontally or vertically between touching squares, can you find a path of 11 squares by applying the operation "+ 7"? For example, a path might go from 12 to 19 (12 + 7 = 19); the next square would then be 26 (19 + 7 = 26), and so on. Now can you find a path of 10 squares by applying the operation "– 9"? This time you may also move to diagonally adjacent squares.

79	86	66	75	85
77	57	64	71	78
68	50	41	32	80
59	43	22	15	23
45	36	29	14	5

LOGIC AND REASONING TASKS 1

The puzzles and exercises in this section build on various core brain skills. Despite appearances, none of them require any mathematics or even general knowledge.

JIGSAW MINI SUDOKU

(solution on page 55)

Can you fit each of the digits 1 to 6 into each row, column and bold-outlined shape of this 6 × 6 grid? You'll definitely need a pen or pencil for this!

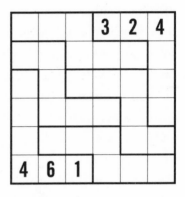

INFERENCES *(solutions on page 55)*

Read each set of statements and then work out whether each conclusion is true or false (that is, unproven).

1 **25 per cent of sweets are made with real fruit juice. Real fruit juice is more expensive than artificial flavouring.**

a Artificially-flavoured sweets are cheaper to buy than those with real fruit juice.

b 75 per cent of sweets are made with artificial flavouring.

2 **Boys under 10 years old never like girls. Girls over 8 years old always like boys.**

a Girls under 8 don't like boys.

b Girls don't like boys who are under 10.

EVIDENTLY LOGICAL *(solution on page 56)*

A terrible crime has been committed at a country mansion. Four cherished objects have vanished from the possession of their loving owner. Can you help solve the mystery of who has borrowed each item based on the witness statements below?

Work out who was last seen with what object and which room they were in at the time. The people, objects and rooms are:

People: Pete, James, Sarah and Kellie
Objects: Pen, Book, Badge and Trophy
Rooms: Hall, Bathroom, Lounge and Kitchen.

- The butler says that he saw a man putting one of the objects in his coat pocket in the hall.
- Kellie was spotted going into the bathroom with an object, but it was definitely not the badge.
- The silver trophy awarded for coming second in the netball was not last seen in the hall or the bathroom.
- The prized quill pen, rumoured to have been used to sign the Declaration of Independence, was last spotted in the kitchen, but not in the possession of either Sarah or Pete.

DOMINOES *(solution on page 56)*

Can you work out how to place a full set of regular dominoes (with 0 for blank) into the following grid?

0	6	1	0	2	2	3	0
0	3	3	6	6	6	3	4
1	4	5	5	5	2	5	3
1	5	0	1	1	2	3	4
5	1	2	4	6	0	4	4
6	2	6	0	5	1	5	4
2	6	1	0	3	2	4	3

Using this tick-off chart may help you to keep track of which dominoes you've already placed.

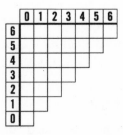

"It is not enough to have a good mind. The main thing is to use it well."

René Descartes (1596–1650)

CARD LOGIC *(solutions on page 56)*

Four double-sided cards are laid out on a table. You can see the following faces:

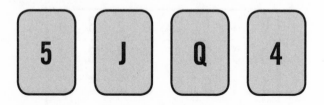

You *know* that each of the cards has a letter on one side and a number on its reverse. You now wish to prove or disprove various assertions.

In each case, what is the minimum number of cards you would need to turn over to prove or disprove the following propositions, and which cards would these be? Consider each of these propositions independently of the others.

- There are precisely two cards with a Q on.
- Every odd-numbered card has a Q on the back.
- All cards with a J on one side have a 4 on the reverse.

MEMORY TASKS 1

By using your memory alone – and not taking notes – try each of the following tasks and see how well you do. You may wish to use a clock or stopwatch to time yourself.

WORD LIST

The following words have no obvious connections, but see how many you can remember after only one minute studying the list. Cover the list and try to reproduce the words in the empty grid below.

Horse	Polygon	Gentle	Meander
Brook	Trio	Plant	Denial

NUMBER GRID

Look at the following arrangement of the numbers 1 to 15 for two minutes. Once the time is up, cover the grid and try to reproduce the numbers on the empty grid below.

6	1	8	2	9
15	11	5	13	14
10	4	7	3	12

MISSING WORDS

Without reading it, cover the bottom list. Now spend 1 minute studying the upper list of words. When the time is up, cover the upper list instead and see if you can spot which words did *not* appear in the original list. The lists are in different orders.

Calculate	Splendid	Gravel	Ultimate
Xylophone	Ingenuity	Dentistry	Topography
Stomach	Altruism	Generality	Tremendous
Diplomat	Underground	Internet	Splendid
Understand	Realize	Intimidate	Abstract

Innumerate	Xylophone	Underground	Calculate
General	Superb	Honesty	Altruism
Stomach	Internet	Abstract	Intimate
Topography	Gravel	Tremendous	Ingenuity
Comprehend	Official	Dentistry	Ultimate

VISUAL MEMORY

Look at the picture, opposite, that is on a grid of dots. Study it for as long as you feel you need to, and then cover it and try to reproduce it as precisely as you can on the empty grid.

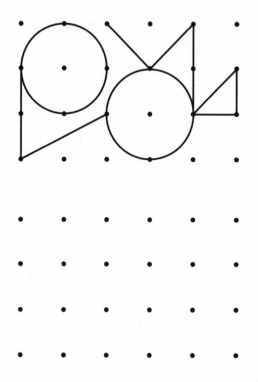

ABSTRACT SEQUENCES

You'll need a sheet of paper again. Start by covering everything except the top row of shapes on the following page, and spend 1 minute memorizing the order. Then cover the top row and uncover the row beneath. Label each shape with a number representing its original position. Write "1" next to the shape that was first in the previous row, and so on. Then try the same with the two other sets of shapes.

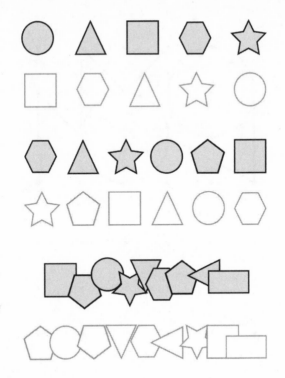

SOLUTIONS: VERBAL

Letter choice

1 EASY
2 TRIAL
3 SOLUTION
4 UNDERSTAND
5 DENIAL
6 TEMERITY
7 HELICOPTER
8 EXALTED

Mixed-up sentences

1 SPEED
2 TREASON
3 STAPLER (or, more esoterically, Psalter!)
4 TAGGED
5 MANGO
6 STERNER
7 INTEGRATION
8 STRAIGHTEN

Synonym sets

joining–combining
proposing–promising
suffering–enduring
ripping–tearing

captivating–entrancing
pending–approaching
developing–growing
tending–caring

Comprehension

1 A dwarf planet
2 24
3 It had not "swept clean" its area of space
4 Chromatic dispersion
5 It is reflected
6 Refraction

Cryptogram

It is never too late to be what you might have been.

George Eliot

Odd-one-out round 1

Prose: the rest are types of poem.

Meter: the rest are types of mathematical average.

Sea: the rest form words when prefixed with "sand".

SOLUTIONS: VISUAL AND SPATIAL
Visual sequences

Line 1 – C: the number of sides increases by 1 each step.

Line 2 – A: each step the triangle rotates anticlockwise; the star rotates clockwise.

Line 3 – C: the two circles rotate anticlockwise.

Reflection

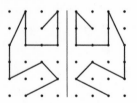

Rotation

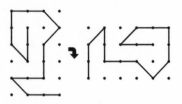

Shape folding

"B" is the only shape that could result from the folding.

Shape counting

14 triangles.

Feature spotting

In your head

- 12 straight edges.
- You could see 7 corners on a cube.
- 3. If the pentagon was not regular, you'd only need 2 triangles.

SOLUTIONS: NUMERICAL

Number sequences

32 Each number is the previous number multiplied by 2.

23 The difference between numbers increases by 1 at each step.

36 The difference increases by 5 from number to number.

243 Each number is the previous one multiplied by 3.

63 Each number is 12 less than the previous one.

Numerical thinking

- 6 eggs: You have 9 after breaking them, and 6 after cooking.
- 21 posts: 2 per metre, and you need one at the start and the end.
- 4 miles: You run 3 miles then walk 1 mile.

Probable problems

- The two heads is most likely, at 1 in 4 – which is 1 in 2 × 1 in 2. The die roll is 1 in 6.
- The card selection is more likely, at 2 in 52 = 1 in 26. The roll of 12 requires a 6 on both dice, which is 1 in 6 × 1 in 6 = 1 in 36.

Time passes

1hr 40min

5hr 50min

18hr 00min

6hr 40min

1hr 11min

This time tomorrow

1 5am today

2 10:30pm yesterday

3 4:20am tomorrow

4 1am today

5 6am tomorrow

6 8am today

A-mazing numbers

79	86	66	75	85
77	57	64	71	78
68	50	41	32	80
59	43	22	15	23
45	36	29	14	5

SOLUTIONS: LOGIC AND REASONING

Jigsaw mini sudoku

6	1	5	3	2	4
1	5	3	2	4	6
5	3	2	4	6	1
3	2	4	6	1	5
2	4	6	1	5	3
4	6	1	5	3	2

Inferences

1a False (not proven). We don't know if the manufacturing cost is tied to the sale price.

1b False. Perhaps some have no flavouring added at all, or something other than fruit juice or artificial flavouring.

2a Not proven – we don't know what girls under 8 think of boys.

2b Not proven – again, we don't know anything about what girls think of boys of different ages.

Evidently logical

Kitchen	Pen	James
Lounge	Trophy	Sarah
Bathroom	Book	Kellie
Hall	Badge	Pete

Dominoes

0	6	1	0	2	2	3	0
0	3	3	6	6	6	3	4
1	4	5	5	5	2	5	3
1	5	0	1	1	2	3	4
5	1	2	4	6	0	4	4
6	2	6	0	5	1	5	4
2	6	1	0	3	2	4	3

Card logic

- The 4 and 5, since you don't yet know what letter is on their backs.
- The 5 and J. If you turn over the Q, it tells you nothing – whether it is even or odd, it will still have a Q on its back. You need to turn over the J to potentially disprove the proposition – if it has an even number on the back, you'll know the statement is false.
- The 5 and J, for similar reasons to the answer above.

3
GETTING FITTER
DAY BY DAY

Understanding how your brain gathers information, and why you need different thinking skills, can help you focus on using your brainpower more effectively. Now that you've had a chance to test the five main areas of mental fitness, this chapter gives you guidance on extending your abilities. It gives you a closer look at each type of skill, and describes how you can benefit by enriching your knowledge and power in these areas.

Improved skills will equip you for the harder exercises in the next chapter but, more importantly, tackling increasingly difficult mind exercises will sharpen your thinking ability in everyday life. Remember that improvements in any skill will produce generalized benefits across your brain, making you smarter in more ways than you might expect!

WORDS AND COMPREHENSION

Words form an integral part of our conscious thoughts, so improving our vocabulary doesn't just make us sound cleverer – it actually enriches our ability to think.

THE POWER OF EXPRESSION

What we perceive in the world around us is coloured by our ability to categorize and describe it to ourselves. It's much easier to describe something accurately if you know the right words. For example, if you know what the word "extrapolation" means ("making a projection, on the basis of information that you already have, in order to define or work out something unknown"), you have access to a concept that is more precise than the familiar "prediction". A richer vocabulary makes it easier to organize your thoughts.

We use words as labels for the things we know, so as we improve our vocabulary we are better able to understand, analyze and appreciate the world around us. For example, we're most likely to use the word "neutrino" if we've already learned what a neutrino is. Learning new words compels us to learn more about the world.

NATURAL LANGUAGE CAPABILITIES

We are all born with innate language abilities. We pick up our powers of hearing and speech in our formative years, so what we are exposed to as a child is of critical importance. If there are certain speech sounds that we don't hear, perhaps because they are not part of the language(s) our parents speak, then we find it hard to distinguish these sounds in later life. It's also much easier to grasp key concepts of grammar and structure as a child.

While learning the basics might be a childhood task for us, improving our richness of expression is a life-long quest. Reading is an excellent source of nourishment for the brain – and reading books or articles on subjects outside our normal experience can be especially beneficial, since it exposes us to unfamiliar words, concepts and facts. This information can help us to make new associations, even between things we already know, and to extend the network of ideas and knowledge in our minds.

IMPROVING YOUR WORD SKILLS

Whether you aim to improve your reading, writing, or speaking and listening skills, certain basic concepts apply throughout. Brevity and structure are important for basic understanding, so when reading, try skimming the text first to get the gist of it. If writing or speaking, keep your phrases brief and make the order easy to follow.

Make notes to remember what you read or hear, and try to find synonyms or alternative ways of expressing yourself when writing or speaking – it will keep what you say interesting while improving its clarity, and it will maintain your mental agility.

Try learning another language, particularly one dissimilar to your own. It is sure to introduce you to new concepts, new ideas and new ways of expressing things.

VISUAL AND SPATIAL SKILLS

Being able to visualize and transform objects in our heads may seem like an artificial exercise, but practising this skill can help with everything from driving through a strange town to planning the layout of your new kitchen.

PICTURES IN YOUR HEAD

Close your eyes and think of a banana. What do you remember first? It's not the taste, even though arguably that's the most useful thing to know about a banana. You probably thought of a curved, yellow object – you may not even have thought explicitly of a fruit. This is because you usually recognize a banana by its appearance.

We are all a lot more visually aware than many of us realize. We remember having seen people before, even if we don't know who they are, and are more likely to identify the outside of a building if we've already been inside it. If we're shown a photograph we took years ago, we're likely to recognize it successfully as our own. This is an amazing ability when we stop to think about the implications – how many thousands of images must we have seen over the years?

TRANSFORMING IMAGES

We can conjure up images in our minds very effectively, but we may find it hard to rotate and transform these images in our heads. This is because we are used to seeing things at particular orientations, so we consider orientation a key component of an object's description. Mostly this is because of gravity – in our real world we know which way up most things will be.

Similarly, we find it hard to imagine what something looks like from above when we look at it from the ground. But in the modern world, spatial awareness is a critical skill. When driving, we must transform our ground-level view into a visualization of what the road would look like if we were staring down from space: when moving at speed, being able to predict upcoming corners and obstacles is essential.

Making sense of reflections is another vital skill – knowing which lane the car in your rear mirror is in could save your life.

IMPROVING YOUR SPATIAL AWARENESS

The following exercises test your visual transformation and your imagination skills – they'll show you just what you're capable of.

• Next time you go on holiday, try imagining how you'd pack your luggage in your car before you actually do this. What is the most efficient way to pack everything in?

- Draw an object purely by looking at its reflection in a mirror, or try copying a simple picture, but drawing it rotated through a quarter turn, or upside down, in relation to the original. Even solving a jigsaw puzzle can give you lots of practice at rotating objects.
- Look at an object, then close your eyes and try to imagine it in detail. Open your eyes again and see what you missed. Try the same experiment later. This also improves your observation skills.
- Visualize folding a piece of paper into an aeroplane shape, then try it out with actual paper. Invent new designs in your head.

IMPROVING YOUR NUMBER SKILLS

Some of us love numbers while others hate them, but we all need to deal with them. Luckily there are various tricks you can apply that can make calculations easier, and even give you the confidence to work out large sums in your head.

THE EFFECT OF NATURE

There wasn't much call for counting beyond single digits for most of our evolutionary past. Perhaps this is why the brain has evolved to be pretty poor when it comes to estimating large numbers, with a weak grasp of anything unusually big. Our intuitive grasp of probability is also poor – as is arguably demonstrated by the existence and popularity of casinos!

MORE OR LESS?

In daily life we often just need an approximation – as a quick check on our change at a store, or to work out if

QUICK RECKONING

Estimating is a good brain exercise as well as a helpful practical skill. It is not only a way of becoming more at ease with manipulating numbers: this type of "educated guesswork" also encourages you to think of different approaches to a question or problem.

Estimate $1 \times 2 \times 3 \times 4 \times 5 \times 6 \times 7 \times 8 \times 9$.

What answer did you give? You probably thought of a number with three or perhaps four digits: maybe 2,000 or so. In fact, the solution is 362,880. If you'd been asked to guess the result of $9 \times 8 \times 7 \times 6 \times 5 \times 4 \times 3 \times 2 \times 1$, you would probably have gone for a larger number, which demonstrates how appalling our instincts are for this sort of thing.

How can you get better at estimating?
- Focus on the most significant (typically the highest) numbers first.
- Round numbers up or down to make them easier to deal with. In the example above, round to the nearest multiple of 10 (ie 5–9 to 10, 1–4 to 0), and ignore the 0s, giving $10 \times 10 \times 10 \times 10 \times 10 = 100,000$ – a much closer estimate.
- When dealing with money, round the digits after the decimal points to whole numbers – so long as they are distributed approximately evenly between low and high fractions, then the overall result will be about right. If they all end in, say, .95, then round everything up and perhaps make a small correction later.

that three-for-two offer on the smaller size is really a good deal. When you don't need a precise answer, don't waste time trying to work one out. But even when you do need precision, being able to estimate whether your calculated answer is sensible is still a worthwhile skill to master. (See p.65.)

CASINO OF THE MIND

If we toss a coin, we get either a "heads" or "tails" result. Whatever the outcome of the coin toss, we can't help but feel that next time we are more likely to get the opposite result. Unfortunately this isn't true. Our brains weren't designed to win at games of chance – instead, they predict results for us based on past experience, namely that the number of heads and tails will be about the same.

The problem is that, while this is a good rule for predicting how the coin will behave on average, it is useless as a predictor of the next result.

We confuse the events of the past with those of the future. Looking forward, there is an excellent chance of getting at least one "heads" in a future 10 tosses (it actually works out at 1,023 in 1,024), but if after 9 of those tosses have been made there have been only "tails", the probability of a "heads" for the 10th toss returns to even (1 in 2). More generally, our brains handle frequencies better than probabilities. We are correct that "heads" and "tails" are equally frequent, so the key is simply to understand that frequencies are best used to model a series of events, not a single one.

PROBABILITIES OF SUCCESS

Probability may seem daunting, but it is really a basic concept. All you need to remember is that the likelihood of an event is equal to the number of ways in which that event can occur, divided by the number of possible outcomes. Thus, the probability of tossing a coin and getting heads is 1 in 2 – ie 1 event (heads) out of 2 possible outcomes (heads and tails). Similarly, when rolling a die, we have 6 equally likely sides, so there is a 1 in 6 chance of rolling a 3. Or if we roll two dice, then there is only one event that gives a total of 12 (6 and 6), out of 36 possible outcomes (6 from the first die multiplied by 6 from the second die), giving a 1/36 probability.

More generally, to find the probability of a sequence of events, simply multiply the individual probabilities together – as in the example above, calculating the dice roll of 12 (1/6 × 1/6 = 1/36). To find the probability of a set of alternatives, add them up – so, for example, the chance of rolling either a 3 or a 4 on one die is 1/6 plus 1/6 = 2/6. Sometimes calculating the opposite, or inverse, event is easier – in this case, simply subtract the inverse event from 1 (the chance of *not* rolling a 3 is 1 *minus* 1/6 = 5/6).

TRANSFORMATIONS

To make handling numbers easier, try the following.

- Simplify problems if you can. If you're multiplying by 6 and then dividing by 2, just multiply by 3 instead (6 divided by 2). Look and think ahead and save yourself unnecessary effort.
- Rearrange problems. For example, when adding, start with the biggest numbers – we find it easier to add small numbers to larger ones than vice versa.
- When estimating the likelihood of a particular event, try extrapolating it to an extreme degree. For example, instead of a single toss of a coin or roll of a die, consider one hundred or even a thousand. This can make trends intuitively easier to see.

FIND SUMS IN EVERYDAY LIFE

Even the most ordinary activities can provide great opportunities for putting your mental agility to the test.

- At the supermarket checkout, try calculating the total in your head before you see the receipt. How close are you to the actual total?
- When driving, estimate fuel consumption or travelling times and average speeds for your journey.

BETTER THINKING, SMARTER REASONING

The key to improving your reasoning skills is to be logical – to start from facts and work out the results step by step. We need to recognize when our instinctive preconceptions may be leading us astray, so we can focus clearly on the truth.

LET LOGIC LEAD THE WAY

The brain is a wonderful learning machine, and it likes nothing better than to recognize patterns and derive associations. Unfortunately, these associations aren't always meaningful. We mistakenly apply generalizations to individuals: for example, we may allow a person's name to colour our perception of them, or when we watch the news on television we find that smartly dressed, telegenic people come across as more believable. We frequently reason backwards, judging entire policies from single sound-bites, or assessing someone's trustworthiness by his or her facial expressions.

To avoid these pitfalls, it helps to be aware of them. When thinking through a subject, check that you're basing your reasoning on observed fact, rather than making assumptions or coming up with vague generalizations and applying them to your individual case.

OVERCOMING INSTINCT

All too often, we jump to conclusions, making snap decisions based on inaccurate premises. We then spend time trying to defend these initial guesses rather than applying reason to a subject. While our instinctive responses may sometimes turn out to be correct, or agree with what we later decide, they are often no more accurate than simply rolling dice. We wildly over-estimate our own ability to be intuitively right, because we get a huge buzz out of being correct, and quickly forget the occasions when we are wrong.

To overcome the impulse to justify your gut instinct, it's much better to try not to come to any conclusions or make any provisional decisions until you've gone through the logic of a situation.

MAKE YOURSELF THINK

Being logical doesn't necessarily mean being laborious – in fact, by clearing away mental clutter, logical thinking can help you work faster and more easily. Rather than blindly ploughing through a problem, look for the big picture and see how you can break it down into simpler tasks. Making notes or drawing diagrams can help. Try to find shortcuts that reduce the amount of work you must do.

Try to apply your experience. See if you can transform the problem to more closely resemble something you've already considered or solved: perhaps you can re-use some of your existing knowledge.

Try looking for inspiration in unexpected places. Deliberately invent stupid solutions – these may suggest fresh approaches. When you watch the news, develop your own opinions on contentious matters. A reporter's opinion isn't always right – in some cases, it may be biased or may be barely more informed than your own. Question everything. Children learn fast about the world through constantly asking "Why?" You can do the same.

TECHNIQUES FOR BETTER MEMORY

A good memory is the ultimate sign of mental fitness. With practice, you can achieve improvements that will last for many years. You can train your short- and long-term memory by applying a few simple, proven techniques.

CONCENTRATION

The key to remembering is to concentrate. The plot of a novel or the argument in a newspaper article can easily elude us if we've been reading with half an eye on the TV. We can even forget where we've parked our car if we're engrossed in other things.

To fix a piece of information in your memory, you need to make a conscious effort, and alert your brain that this is worth remembering. Try saying it out loud, writing it down or underlining it – you'll soon find a method that works for you. Then go back over the information later to reinforce the memory. And again later still. It's well worth challenging yourself to remember things you might normally write down, such as travel directions, shopping lists, phone numbers, and even names of people.

MAKE CONNECTIONS

You already know a lot about the world. If you can make connections to this existing knowledge, then you'll be able to reduce the amount of new information you need to learn. This can work in many different ways for the various types of thing you may wish to remember.

If you want to remember what something looks like, try to spot a similarity with an existing object and make that connection. To remember a person's name, try to link their appearance with their name – for example, if they have a beard and their name is Dave, think "Dave-no-shave". If the idea is daft, so much the better.

MAKE IT RELEVANT

In Chapter 1 we saw how strong emotions help memories stick, owing to the way our brains flag things as important. We remember emotive writing far better

NUMBER CRUNCHING
Making connections works even for lists of digits. Break a number into smaller sequences that mean something to you. In this way you'll reduce the quantity of items to remember, particularly if you can make one memory automatically trigger the next. For example, I might remember the number 421975 as "the meaning of life (according to *The Hitchhiker's Guide to the Galaxy*): 42" and "the year I was born: 1975". Now "the meaning of life is me being born" is all I need to recall 421975 – and the humour in this rather ridiculous proposition makes it stick all the better.

than facts, which is why we can recall stories we've enjoyed years after we first heard them, and yet sometimes forget almost everything we've only just read. To remember items that you read in newspapers or watch on TV, try imagining how you might feel if these issues affected or involved you. By deliberately connecting information that you wish to recall to your emotions, you can help convince your brain to transfer it to long-term memory.

4
INTERMEDIATE EXERCISES

In this new workout, you'll be revisiting the same skills that you tested in Chapter 2, but the challenges are now more involved. Try to set aside regular amounts of time during which you won't be distracted, so that you can devote your attention to these puzzles. Remember that focus is an important part of successful thinking. Again, the solutions are given at the end of the chapter, and many of them also contain explanations of how to arrive at the answer. If you found any of the puzzles difficult or even if you were unable to solve them, study the solution and then try the puzzle again – this can be an effective way to fix a new problem-solving technique in your mind.

VERBAL TASKS 2

It's time to put your improved word skills to the test.

PHRASE FINDER (solutions on page 93)

Six proverbs have been written below, but only the first letter of each word has been given. Can you work out what the proverbs are?

1 A S I T S N
2 B L T N
3 T M C S T B

4 T C T A C
5 A B I T H I W T I T B
6 T E B C T W

LETTERS FROM SPACE (solutions on page 93)

In each of these somewhat unusual sentences a single letter has been replaced by a question mark, and all the spaces have been removed. Can you work out what each of the original sentences was?

1 ?hilli??laysthebag?i?eswith?ro?era??etite

2 ?wi??eringblue?i?s?winwi?h?rumpe?sfor?onal?rea?s

3 ?a??ymi??e??ayba??i?a?ure?ucce??forafu??y?upper

4 ?o??eringol??a??yis?rea?ing?ay?reams

5 ?b?n?n??nd?n??rdv?rk?re?ll?nnc?np?int

BROKEN WORDS (solutions on page 93)

The letter fragments on each of the lines at the top of the opposite page can be rearranged and assembled to make a word. Can you stick the words back together?

1	TUS	RA	PA	AP	
2	ULT	FF	IC	DI	
3	DO	AN	TE	TI	
4	EN	TI	IM	CE	PA
5	ND	ENT	TRA	NS	CE

ODD-ONE-OUT ROUND 2 *(solutions on page 94)*

In each of these sets of words, can you spot which is the odd one out? No general knowledge is required to solve this challenge.

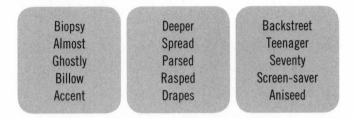

Biopsy	Deeper	Backstreet
Almost	Spread	Teenager
Ghostly	Parsed	Seventy
Billow	Rasped	Screen-saver
Accent	Drapes	Aniseed

EVERY LETTER COUNTS *(solutions on page 94)*

How accurately can you skim-read words? In the following phrases, count how many times the bold letter occurs – as fast as you can.

S A solo soprano sings softly.

B Babbling brooks bring beautiful breezes.

D Independence and gladness meld in a dryad's dreams.

T The temerity to treat is, in truth, totally taught.

E Every letter ends in an E.

L All eligible girls call gullibility appalling, actually.

WORD UP *(solutions on page 94)*

Can you climb each of these word ladders? Travel from the bottom to the top rung by changing just one letter per step. For example, you could climb from COME to GONE via a step labelled CONE.

DOG		WELL		GOLD		DEFT
CAT				BARS		
		DONE				
						PASS

DO YOU GET ME? *(solutions on page 94)*

Read the passage just once and then see if you can answer the questions below.

I love modern art – abstract painting. Much better than everything older: that's all rubbish. Except for really ancient art – I'm fascinated by Egyptian hieroglyphics. I'm particularly into their Middle Kingdom, from about 2000 to 1750 BC – that's the 11th and 12th Dynasties. I'm not interested in the later ones. The Egyptians kept purple as a royal colour – I love anything purple.

1 What is my opinion of 17th-century Dutch masters' paintings?
2 What is my opinion of the 15th Dynasty?
3 What dynastic kingdom is the year 1875 BC classified into?

4 What is it about Egyptian art that I like?

5 Do I like violets?

VISUAL AND SPATIAL TASKS 2

Try to solve these tasks without using a pen or pencil, and without rotating the book or using a mirror.

SPOT THE ROTATION *(solution on page 94)*

Look at the picture on the right.
If you were to rotate this by half
a revolution (180º), which of the
images below would result?

A   **B**   **C**

SPOT THE REFLECTION *(solution on page 95)*

Which of the three lower images
would you see if you were to look at
the picture on the right in a mirror?

A   **B**   **C**

SHAPE COUNTING *(solutions on page 95)*

Look at this grid of shapes, and then answer the questions below as quickly as you can. This tests visual recognition skills, concentration and memory.

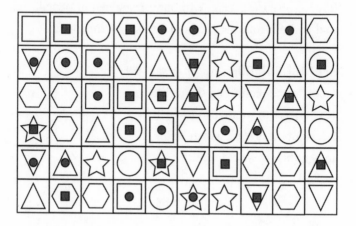

1 How many different combinations of inner and outer shape can you find? Count upright and inverted triangles as different shapes.

2 How many rows or columns have three or more of the same outer shape?

3 How many pairs of matching horizontally or vertically adjacent inner shapes are there?

4 How many circles are immediately adjacent to a square? Count both inner and outer shapes when working this out.

5 How many rows or columns *don't* have at least one circle, triangle, star, square and hexagon of any size or orientation?

UPSIDE-DOWN DIFFERENCES *(solutions on page 95)*

Try to find all 10 differences between these two mirror images.

A-MAZING SHAPES *(solutions on page 96)*

Can you negotiate your way from start to finish through this maze? Start on the bottom left square and move to any square in the same row or column which has either the same *shape* or the same *number*. Then repeat this from each new square until you reach the top right.

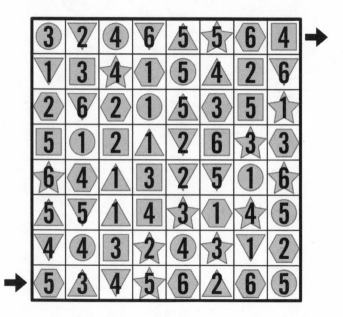

For an even tougher challenge, can you find the minimum number of moves from square to matching square that are required to get through the maze?

NUMERICAL TASKS 2

Time to divide, multiply, and hopefully conquer.

GROUP BY NUMBER *(solutions on page 96)*

How many sequences of adjacent numbers can you find in the following list that each add up to 10? (For example, 3 4 3 near the start.)

1 3 4 3 3 2 5 8 4 3 9 2 5 4 3 2 5 1 6 3 7 8 2 2 5 3 1 1 4 6 5 8 3 2

And how many sequences that multiply to make 20 or 30 can you find?

BALANCE THE FORCE *(solutions on page 97)*

On the diagram below, the grey boxes represent five weights of 1, 2, 3, 4 and 7 grams. The orange triangle is a fulcrum (centre of balance). The effect of each weight is proportional to its distance from the fulcrum times the value of the weight itself. So, for example, the effect of a 2-gram weight on the left-most column (4 units from the centre) would be 4 units × 2 grams = 8. Label each of the grey boxes with one of the five given weights so that both sides will be in equilibrium.

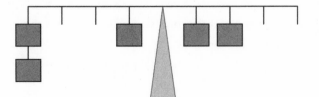

(DON'T) QUANTIFY THIS *(solutions on page 97)*

How quickly can you sort each of these groups into increasing numeric order? Write 1, 2, 3 and so on next to each item in the group, to indicate your decisions. In some cases, you'll be able to do it faster if you only estimate the values.

1 Half of 12   40% of 99   Twice 20   25% of 50

2 1×3 $2 + 4$ 5×7 3×8
   $4 - 2$ 9×1 5×5

3 $3 + 4 + 5$ $3 \times 4 \times 5$ $5 - 4 + 3$ $3 + 4 - 5$
   $3 \times (4 + 5)$ $(3 + 4) \times 5$

4 42×3 145×735 $265 + 1,240$ 132×99
   $10,243$

LUCKY NUMBER DIP *(solutions on page 98)*

Refer to the following set of numbers to find answers to the questions below them:

3   8   12   17   21   24   25

1 Can you find two numbers that add up to the value of a third number?

2 Can you find two numbers that multiply to give a third number?

3 How many of these numbers are prime (only divisible by themselves and 1)?

4 What is the sum of all seven numbers?

5 How many of the numbers are multiples of 3 or 7?

A HEAD FOR HEIGHTS – AND FIGURES *(solution on page 98)*

Can you finish building this number pyramid? Each brick in the pyramid must contain a number equal to the sum of the two bricks directly beneath it. For example, the 5 at the bottom right already has a 2 beneath it, so the other empty square below it must be a 3.

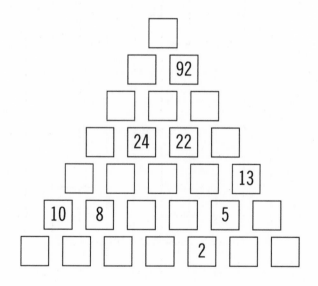

LOGIC AND REASONING TASKS 2

This time you'll face some more complex challenges.

SOME ASSEMBLY REQUIRED *(solutions on pages 98–9)*

Can you fill each tetromino (set of four squares) with circles, stars or triangles so that no two tetrominoes filled with the same shape touch?

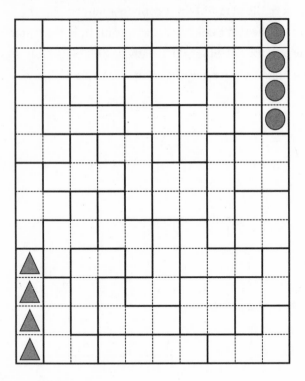

LOOP THE LOOP *(solution on page 99)*

Can you complete this Slitherlink puzzle? You must join adjacent dots with horizontal or vertical lines, such that every square with a number in it must have lines around that number of its four sides. The aim is to draw one big closed loop: this loop cannot touch or cross itself, and there must be no loose ends or disconnected sections.

The example shown below should help to clarify the rules:

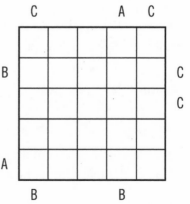

AS EASY AS A, B, C *(solution on page 100)*

Can you fit the letters A, B and C once each into every row and column of this grid? Some squares will be empty. Letters outside the grid show which letter is closest to that end of the relevant row or column. For example, B is the first letter reading across the 2nd row.

THINKING CAP *(solutions on page 100)*

Read the following statements, then for each statement decide which of the conclusions are correct and which are unproven assertions.

1 **I toss a particular coin 25 times and I get heads every time.**

a The coin has heads on both sides.

b I am very lucky.

2 **I am standing in the shade and the sun is in the east.**

a My shadow is to the west of me.

b It is morning.

DOWN IN THE ORCHARD *(solution on page 100)*

Five farmers are planning their fruit picking. On the basis of the statements below, work out who harvests which fruit in what month.

Farmers:	Black, Giles, Jones, Smith, White
Fruit:	Apples, Cherries, Oranges, Raspberries, Strawberries
Months:	June, July, August, September, October

- The raspberries are harvested later than the strawberries.
- Farmer Giles, who is not the cherry farmer, picks his fruit earlier than Farmer Jones.

- The cherries are picked before Farmer Smith's strawberries are picked.
- Farmer Black, who doesn't grow apples, picks in August.
- The October harvest is of oranges, but is not Farmer White's.

MEMORY TASKS 2

It's time to test your powers of recall – not just for words, but for numbers and shapes, too. You'll need a timer.

NUMBER GRID

Look at the following grid, containing the numbers 1 to 20, for two minutes. Once the time is up, cover the numbers and try to reproduce their arrangement in the empty grid below. It may help to look for patterns by noting how numbers are positioned relative to each other.

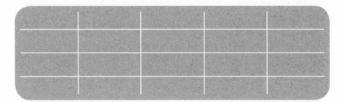

12	18	8	7	5
19	13	16	1	2
9	15	11	10	17
14	20	4	3	6

WORD ORDER

Cover the page below the grid of words. Study the words for two minutes, then cover them and reveal the empty grid. Below it are the words in a different order. Write them in the grid in their original order.

Derogatory	Truancy	Objectify	Demonstrate
Remonstrate	Dignity	Transformation	Interlude
Travesty	Entertainment	Intercutting	Sophistry
Invoice	Obfuscation	Sesquipedalian	Entity

Intercutting sesquipedalian obfuscation; sophistry – entertainment entity. Demonstrate truancy. Objectify derogatory travesty! Remonstrate dignity. Transformation, interlude. Invoice.

SHAPE-ING UP

Study this set of shapes for two minutes, then cover it.

Now look at the rotated versions above. How many of the shapes are missing? Can you draw the missing shapes?

MEMORY DIS-PAIR

Study the box of semi-related word pairs for up to one minute. Then cover this box and look at the one below it, which has just one word from each pair. Can you recall the second word in the pair?

Apple & Orange	Carrot & Pumpkin
Front & Right	North & West
Exterior & External	Triumph & Victory
Upset & Worry	Investigate & Nose
Down & Descent	Blue & Ultraviolet
Triumvirate & Duality	Central & Excluded

Investigate	Carrot
West	Descent
Apple	Right
Exterior	Central
Worry	Triumph
Blue	Duality

VISUAL MEMORY

Study the pattern on the left for one minute, then cover it and reproduce as much of it as you can on the empty grid to the right.

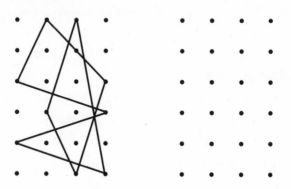

I'VE LOST MY (OBJECT)

Cover the page under the following grid of words. Study the words for as long as you feel you need; then cover the grid and spot the missing items from the list beneath, which is otherwise in the same order.

ID card	Spanner	Hamster	Lamp
Chair	Postbox	Pencil	Goldfish
Racing car	Camera	Bamboo	Telephone
Book	The Moon	Apple	Monkey

Which objects are missing from the following list?
Spanner, Chair, Postbox, Racing car, Telephone, Book, Apple, Monkey

SOLUTIONS: VERBAL

Phrase finder

1 A stitch in time saves nine
2 Better late than never
3 Too many cooks spoil the broth
4 Two's company, three's a crowd
5 A bird in the hand is worth two in the bush
6 The early bird catches the worm

Letters from space

1 ?=P: Phillip plays the bagpipes with proper appetite
2 ?=T: Twittering bluetits twin with trumpets for tonal treats
3 ?=S: Sassy misses say bass is a sure success for a fussy supper
4 ?=D: Doddering old daddy is dreading daydreams
5 ?=A: A banana and an aardvark are all Ann can paint

Broken words

1 APPARATUS
2 DIFFICULT
3 ANTIDOTE
4 IMPATIENCE
5 TRANSCENDENT

Odd-one-out round 2

Ghostly: all the other words have their letters in alphabetical order.

Deeper: the rest are all anagrams of each other.

Seventy: all the rest contain a double e: "ee".

Every letter counts

S=5, B=7, D=8, T=12, E=6, L=14

Word up

DOG → DOT → COT → CAT

WELL → DELL → DOLL → DOLE → DONE

GOLD → BOLD → BALD → BARD → BARS

DEFT → LEFT → LEST → PEST → PAST → PASS

The last ladder has several solutions. One is the sequence shown above. See how many others you can find.

Do you get me?

1 I think they're rubbish. (They're old art.)

2 I'm not interested. (It's a later dynasty.)

3 Middle Kingdom.

4 The hieroglyphics.

5 Yes (I love anything purple).

SOLUTIONS: VISUAL AND SPATIAL

Spot the rotation

B It is not C because the stars are stacked in the wrong order.

Spot the reflection

A In B and C the "shell" or "antenna" are facing the wrong way.

Shape counting

1 There are 12 combinations of inner and outer shape, plus 6 shapes with no inner shape. This is easier to count if you start with each outer shape and scan for different inner shapes.

2 5 rows (all but the penultimate) and 2 columns (the 2nd and 7th).

3 10 times (7 in the rows, 3 in the columns).

4 20, including counting both circles in cells with inner *and* outer circles.

5 1 row and 5 columns. This is much easier if you check for hexagons first, then stars, as these are much rarer.

Upside-down differences

A-mazing shapes

The shortest solution uses 15 steps. One possibility is:

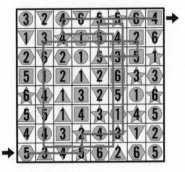

SOLUTIONS: NUMERICAL

Group by number

10 sequences that add up to 10:

3 + 4 + 3

4 + 3 + 3

3 + 2 + 5

3 + 2 + 5

1 + 6 + 3

3 + 7

8 + 2

2 + 5 + 3

5 + 3 + 1 + 1

4 + 6

9 sequences that multiply to 20 and 30. For 20:

5 × 4

2 × 2 × 5

For 30:

$3 \times 2 \times 5$

$3 \times 2 \times 5$

$5 \times 1 \times 6$

$2 \times 5 \times 3$

$2 \times 5 \times 3 \times 1$

$2 \times 5 \times 3 \times 1 \times 1$

6×5

Balance the force

There are two possible solutions to this puzzle:

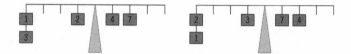

(Don't) quantify this

1 The order is 1, 3, 4, 2. Don't calculate 40% of 99 – you need only note that it must be (slightly) less than "twice 20".

2 The order is 2, 3, 7, 5, 1, 4, 6.

3 The order is 3, 6, 2, 1, 4, 5.

4 The order is 1, 5, 2, 4, 3. Again, don't calculate these. The second number (145×735) is clearly the largest. Then 132×99 must be very close to the value of 132×100 – either way, it is notably more than 10,243. The rest then fall into place.

Lucky number dip

1 8 + 17 = 25

2 3 × 8 = 24

3 2: 3 and 17

4 110

5 4: 3, 12, 21, 24.

A head for heights – and figures

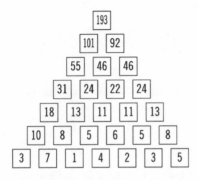

SOLUTIONS: LOGIC AND REASONING
Some assembly required

This puzzle is actually very easy. There are only two possible arrangements of circle and star next to the triangles at the bottom left – one works and one doesn't. Even with trial and error, it takes less than a minute to see which one works. Alternatively, you can use a label for "either circles or stars", say "x", and write this in across the puzzle, alternating with triangles where appropriate. At the top right, you will have placed the triangles next to the circles, and the puzzle is effectively solved. You can then simply work back again, changing the "x"s to stars or circles as appropriate. Either way, the key is to start next to one of the known shapes.

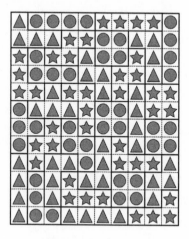

Loop the loop

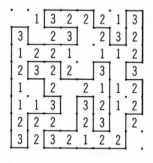

As easy as A, B, C

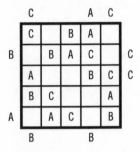

Thinking cap

1a Not proven. I might just be lucky.

1b Also not proven. The coin might have heads on both sides – and, in any case, the definition of "lucky" depends on the circumstances.

(The two options are both possible explanations, but neither is proven.)

2a Not proven. I am in the shade so I have no shadow.

2b Proven, no matter where you are on Earth.

Down in the orchard

June	Cherries	White
July	Strawberries	Smith
August	Raspberries	Black
September	Apples	Giles
October	Oranges	Jones

INTERLUDE

A PUZZLING HISTORY

Puzzles appear every day in newspapers and magazines throughout the world, and their range and variety continue to increase. In fact, puzzles have fascinated us for thousands of years.

RIDDLE ME THIS

Riddles appear in the Book of Judges – part of both the Hebrew Bible and the Christian Old Testament, dating from at least 1,000BC. Greek philosophers also posed elaborate riddles, including the well-known Riddle of the Sphinx in Sophocles' play *Oedipus Tyrannus*, first performed around 430BC.

Riddles were based on logic and word play, with examples often found in early writings, such as this riddle from 1st-millennium Old English poetry: "What thief in the dark digests the words of man and their foundation, and yet remains no wiser for having swallowed these words?" The answer is a bookworm – riddles use double meanings, such as "in the dark" referring to both actual darkness and ignorance.

THE PURSUIT OF LEISURE

More recently, in the last few centuries, an increasingly industrialized society led to greater amounts of leisure time, so many people began to find time to spend on trivia and curiosities. Some of these were toys and games such as mechanical sliding block puzzles; but with improved literacy and cheap printing, puzzles also started to be regular fixtures in magazines and journals.

The author Lewis Carroll (*Alice's Adventures in Wonderland*) – real name Charles Lutwidge Dodgson – was fascinated by the ways words and numbers could be manipulated. He incorporated picture puzzles in letters he wrote, replacing words or syllables with images that, with suitable interpretation, could be pronounced the same way. Similar to the ancient Egyptian hieroglyphic writing system, such picture puzzles had been popular in the 18th century, when the letter-writing classes included them in their missives. Carroll also invented, or at least popularized, word ladders (see p.78), and proposed a word game with movable letter tiles, rather like Scrabble™. He was a mathematics lecturer at Oxford University, so it's no surprise that he also devised a wide range of fiendish maths puzzles.

FROM WORD SQUARES TO CROSSWORDS

As printing technologies advanced, puzzles that used more complex layouts began to be developed. Puzzles involving fitting letters into a grid of squares had been around for centuries, but the first published crossword is generally accredited to Arthur Wynne, whose Word-Cross appeared in *New York World* in 1913. Within a few years, crosswords started to spread and by the middle of the 20th century were well and truly established, published daily in newspapers across the globe.

The *Sunday Express* introduced crosswords to UK newspapers in 1924. When the *Times* of London finally bowed to reader pressure and added its own crossword in 1930, just a month later the newspaper felt compelled to offer an additional Latin crossword – with both clues and answers in Latin – to satisfy some of its readers, who had "hitherto shunned the English" version as failing to meet their "exacting intellectual standard". A prescient editorial on 1 March 1930 noted the psychological addictiveness of the "gradual and growing joy of seeing white square after white square getting nicely filled in", and even pre-shadowed the development of brain-training by describing crosswords as an "agreeable mental exercise" that provides the "stimulus of feeling oneself a clever fellow".

MODERN PUZZLES

The perfect exemplar of the modern puzzle is Sudoku. Despite its Japanese name, meaning "single number", Sudoku was actually invented in the US in 1979 by an architect called Howard Garns. Based on a grid, requiring no knowledge, and able to be completed (with practice) in mere minutes, Sudoku is truly egalitarian, liberated from the constraints of society, education and language. Despite its origin, it was initially most successful in Japan, where its language-independent nature made it an attractive alternative to word puzzles in a country with an alphabet of more than 1,000 letters. Its eventual worldwide popularity began when it was introduced by the *Times* of London in 2004 – within weeks it was in newspapers across the globe.

Another example is Kakuro, named in Japan but again invented in the US. Essentially a crossword with numbers and the digit-placing rules from Sudoku, it is said to be the best-selling puzzle in Japan. Other Sudoku variant puzzles have also become popular in their own right, such as Killer Sudoku (Kakuro on a Sudoku grid) and Futoshiki (Sudoku with "less than" or "greater than" symbols as clues). These led to Japanese publishers developing a range of their own language-free logic puzzles, all based on filling in grids with numbers, shading, lines or loops, such as the Slitherlink puzzles in this book.

In a further development, the advent of sophisticated mobile phones has enabled many people around the world to tackle puzzles interactively within phone apps, introducing a social aspect that includes comparing solving times and difficulty ratings.

5
ADVANCED
MENTAL SKILLS

Puzzles are fun, but they needn't be just games – they can be of real benefit in training your mind. If you were to "deconstruct" what your brain was doing as it solved a Sudoku or a crossword, you might be amazed at the different thinking modes that come into play. Many of the skills honed over a paper puzzle will stand you in good stead when writing a top-grade essay, putting together a cogent argument for a meeting, or fathoming a politician's logic. If you seek to gain rapid proficiency at particular puzzles, there are countless books and websites to teach you special techniques – but working out these methods for yourself is perhaps the ultimate test of your ingenuity, and it's much more rewarding!

You'll have noticed that your brain seems to work better in some circumstances than others. This chapter provides advice on how to break through any blockages and shows you how to apply your sharpened mental capabilities in many areas of everyday life.

REASONING AND DECISION-MAKING

Learning to use your brain more effectively is a mix of science and art. By applying the skills covered in this book, you can rapidly find and understand the essence of a problem, then make faster and better decisions.

STRATEGIES FOR SUCCESS

Real-life decision-making typically requires a mix of abilities: not just logical thinking but also numeric, verbal, memory and creative skills. This intermingling of skills mirrors the interconnected nature of the brain, with the act of being "creative" distributed across them all.

Your brain is already capable of creative leaps of inspiration – you just need to let it get to work. The 19th-century thinker Henri Poincaré broke the creative process down into four steps: preparation, incubation, illumination and verification. Preparation involves logically analyzing and breaking down the task, as shown in the puzzles on the following pages. Incubation is the art of letting your subconscious mind work, as discussed on pages 118–9. These lead to illumination – the wonderful "aha!" moment when your brain is rewarded for its efforts – and then finally verification of the solution.

If illumination doesn't come along immediately, give it time. Expect frustration, and don't pressure yourself. Try imagining ridiculous solutions, or make guesses and see what conflicts they might lead to, or try describing the problem differently – in terms of formal logic, for example.

Finally, don't forget verification. Check your solution: if it's wrong, then work out why. If you're tackling a puzzle with a known answer like those in this book, then work out why the given answer is correct. And if you were right, give your brain the satisfaction of knowing this.

A QUESTION OF LOGIC

Expressing a problem in a formal logical fashion is the ultimate way to strip it down to its essentials. It might sound complex, but it simply involves presenting an argument as a set of propositions with symbols to show the relationships between them. To see how this can work, first try solving the following problem without making any notes or reading on:

A red sky at night means it will always be dry the next morning, but it is only ever hot the next morning if there is a red sky at night accompanied by a Westerly wind. When it is dry the next morning, however, there is never a Westerly wind the previous night. If there is a red sky tonight, will it be hot tomorrow?

We can rewrite the problem by labelling each proposition as a letter:

A = "a red sky at night"   B = "dry tomorrow"
C = "a Westerly wind"   D = "hot tomorrow"

Now by using —> to mean "implies" we can write:
A —> B   D —> A & C   B —> not C

So the question becomes, "If A, what state is D in?"
We can follow a chain of logical implications and see that:
A —> B —> not C
So D cannot be true because if it were then both A and C would be true.
Therefore the answer is "No, it won't be hot tomorrow."

SUDOKU BUILDS YOUR BRAIN

Sudoku is a pure logic puzzle, requiring no world knowledge, language, or even mathematical skills. It demonstrates how applying logical, step-by-step thinking can turn an intimidating problem into an enjoyable exercise.

THE AIM OF THE GAME

In Sudoku, you must place each of the digits 1 to 9 into every row, column and bold-lined 3 × 3 box of a 9 × 9 grid. Despite this simple premise, there is a great deal of depth to the puzzle.

Let's look at a sample grid:

				5				
			8		7			
	3	1		☆		8	6	
8				3				5
		3				7		⬡
2				4				8
	2	7		☆		6	4	
			1		2			
				9				

MAKING A PLAN

The first thing to realize is that the digits have no actual value. You could use nine colours instead, for example, and this might even make it easier to spot patterns. We can make some further initial observations:

- To place all the digits 1 to 9 into each row, column and 3 × 3 box, you can use each digit only once in each of these areas. This observation is central: without it, the deductive eliminations necessary to progress cannot be made. In any puzzle or task, it is important to define your starting point accurately so you can derive the correct implications and requirements.

- Some rows and columns have more pre-placed digits than others.

- Some pre-placed digits occur more often than other digits.

- Guessing is not a promising strategy – there are 59 empty squares, and the possible entries for each range from 1 to 9.

A SERIES OF ELIMINATIONS

Now, you need to find a starting place. A good strategy is to identify parts of the puzzle that provide the most information. Remember that all of the squares are constrained: only the digits 1 to 9 can fit in them. Look for the rows, columns and boxes with the most numbers already in place. Here, the most constrained squares, with the fewest valid possible entries, are the two marked with stars. To understand why, count how many numbers can be "seen" from these squares. As this puzzle is symmetrical, finding the entry for one starred square will give you a further clue for the other – its symmetric opposite.

Each square solved adds to your knowledge about the remaining empty squares, thus enabling you to form a chain of successive observations and eliminations. So long as each step is entirely logical, you can have complete confidence in the resulting solution.

THE POWER OF PATTERNS

In the right-most three columns we already have two 6s, and observation shows that the only place a 6 can fit in the remaining column is the square marked with a hexagon. Applying this logic again, we can look for other regions where a particular number has been eliminated from all but one square.

Solving a Sudoku puzzle involves spotting "patterns" that can direct you to logical conclusions, perhaps in instances where making deductions would otherwise be less easy. For example, if an area has just three empty squares and two of those squares have the same two possible candidates, the third square must hold the remaining number. It's also worth noting that a good working memory will help make you faster at Sudoku, making it easier to remember which digits you have already seen or just placed. Practise noting which digits are missing from a row, column or box simply by glancing.

NARROW YOUR SEARCH SPACE

Most logical problems can be defined as a *search* for a solution – and involve knowing how to look as well as what to look for. Sudoku is a good example. You could write in every possible digit for every square, and then gradually cancel out all the "wrong" entries. If you're truly stuck or have a limited number of possibilities this approach may have some merit, but more usually it results in information overload that actually makes it harder to spot salient facts. In many ways this is a "brute force" method, rather as a computer might be programmed to solve problems. But we are not computers: we can think.

Writing in all possible digits on the sample Sudoku

HOW SUDOKU TONES YOUR BRAIN

Being able to skim and analyze information rapidly will help with a wide range of tasks. Sudoku:

- Teaches you to look at what is actually being asked or presented in a problem, rather than being misled by appearances – at first glance Sudoku might look like a mathematical nightmare, but in fact no mathematical skills are necessary
- Helps to enhance logical, deductive thinking
- Improves your working memory, building up your ability to hold and manipulate information in your mind.

would have revealed 2 as the only candidate for the upper starred square, but it would have taken much longer and been less efficient. When searching for an answer, don't just blindly churn through all the possibilities. Step back and think, then focus your effort where you're most likely to make progress.

You can apply this process in everyday life, too. For example, when you search online for an article you'll first need to define what you're looking for, otherwise you'll end up with too many possibilities. Similarly, when reasoning you should set yourself the tightest possible parameters to guide your search for an answer.

CROSSWORDS MAKE YOU CLEVERER

Crosswords are great all-round workouts for the mind, drawing on word skills, memory and logic. They also help enrich vocabulary and hone the ability to think creatively.

A CORNUCOPIA OF CROSSWORDS

There are many styles of crossword, which vary in difficulty and size, but they are all based on a grid of squares. Part of a grid is shown on the opposite page. You solve it by working out clues and filling in horizontal (across) and vertical (down) answers. Many squares form part of both an across and a down answer; a good crossword has lots of these squares, which help you to fill in further answers.

In "straight" clues, often the answer is a simple

synonym of the clue. Some crosswords are "cryptic":
in these, answers may be hidden inside some of the clue
words, may include abbreviations such as "N" for "north"
or words that sound like the answer, or may be an
anagram of some of the clue words, with the rest of the
clue giving a "pointer" to the anagram.

GETTING STARTED

Try to solve the clues that reveal the most about the
rest of the grid. Aim for longer answers first, especially
those that will provide the most initial letters for other
answers. In a cryptic crossword, seek out anagram clues,
where the solution is most precisely defined.

Most crosswords have a few relatively easy clues to get
you going, so skim through the whole set first rather than
struggling on a few. If you can't think of an answer, move
on to a different clue. Your unconscious mind may carry
on processing, ready for when you return to it (see p.118).
You can use the same approach when tackling problems
such as an exam – assess the task as a whole, then tackle
the easy bits and build up to the harder ones. Early

This long answer
at the top of the
grid gives you the
initial letters for
four other clues

Short or very long
words are more
distinctive, and can
be easier to solve

¹M	A	²R	B	³L	E
6	7				
10			11		12

mistakes can greatly slow your progress. Remember to challenge your earlier assumptions if you get stuck.

MAKING THE MOST OF YOUR MEMORY

The brain indexes words the way we most often need them, starting with the first character – we've all had that "tip of the tongue" feeling where we know a word but can only recall the first letter. It's therefore much easier to solve a clue if you have the first letter. The last letter is surprisingly important, too. Try reading this: "I hvae ltlite turolbe minkag snsee of tihs setanmtet." Although only the first and last letters are in the correct order, the "sneentce" is still intelligible.

Understanding how we index and retrieve words can help in other ways. When solving anagrams, your brain can sometimes mislead you, seizing on groups that look like bits of words and restricting your choice of possible answers. Anagrams that form words in themselves, like those on pages 33 and 34, are particularly deceptive. To break these patterns, jumble up letters by writing them in a circle or at random, so you aren't misled by partial word matches. The opposite process can also be useful when you're trying to think creatively – word fragments and even single letters can trigger all sorts of ideas.

CREATIVE THINKING

Synonyms or alternative meanings are at the heart of the typical clue, and they're a great test of thinking

HOW CROSSWORDS TONE YOUR BRAIN

Crosswords are excellent for building your vocabulary and comprehension skills. These puzzles can also give your memory and deductive abilities a workout. They can:

- Teach you to break a problem down into its constituent parts, and organize a method of working through it
- Help you to challenge assumptions in your thinking, so you keep track of what is certain and what is simply probable
- Help to improve logical, deductive thinking
- Train you to think "outside the box" and generate new ideas
- Encourage you to remember any new words or facts, or alternative word meanings, that you work out, thanks to your focused attention and the reward of finally discovering the answer!

skills. Many words have multiple meanings, so be sure to consider all the possibilities for a given clue. Practice in solving crosswords makes it easier to spot alternative meanings in future, particularly if you experience an "aha!" moment. Once you realize that a "flower" can be a flow-er – a river – and not just a plant, for example, you'll easily remember that interpretation next time. You're wiring up your brain for a different kind of recall.

Sometimes we find it hard to retrieve the alternative meanings of a word, if we've focused our attention on one possible meaning. Our brains don't want us to get muddled, so they block the competing interpretations. To free up your mind, try reading a clue aloud, or having it read to you – this might suggest a new interpretation.

The need to pronounce it and listen to it forces you to reassess the clue and activate the retrieval process via a different part of your brain.

APPLYING LOGIC

You may find it easiest to solve clues for particularly short or long words, simply because there are fewer words that can fit. In English, there are more 8- and 9-letter words than words of any other length, so leave these until later.

For some clues, you might not yet know the complete answer, but perhaps you can solve some of it. Try placing some likely letters and see if they help trigger your memory. If you have some letters placed already, then where are the vowels likely to be? Maybe you can deduce the prefix or suffix of a word, such as RE– or –ING, so write or pencil this in to help with other clues. Is the word singular or plural? What part of speech is it? Is it a synonym, or a name or a place? Use deductive logic to narrow your options.

TACKLING PROBLEMS

Whether you're dealing with a puzzle or with an issue in daily life, sometimes you'll get stuck. Luckily, there are various tactics that can be used to "jump-start" your thinking.

TRIGGER YOUR SUBCONSCIOUS

Have you ever returned from a break and made sudden progress on a particularly knotty problem? Sometimes this may have been because you forgot your preconceptions and found a fresh perspective. But on other occasions it was evidence that your unconscious mind had been quietly processing and reorganizing your thoughts for you.

A quick way to stimulate your subconscious is by describing your problem out loud. Explaining something to yourself or another person is a great way to find holes in arguments. As you speak, you often think of new ideas or possible solutions.

WHEN IT'S RIGHT TO BE WRONG

With some problems, starting from a reasonable initial guess is helpful, even if your guess turns out to be wrong.

THE MAGIC OF SLEEP

Sleep doesn't just give our bodies a chance to rest. It can also be a vital part of the thinking process, by allowing our subconscious mind to work (see opposite). When we sleep, we usually dream, whether we remember it or not. In dreams, our brains rehearse what we have done during the day, learning from and filing away the day's events. We also think while we dream – in fact, we use almost as much energy as when we're awake, so busy is the brain with its housekeeping. So next time you're struggling with a problem, make sure you have a good night's sleep, or even just a quick nap, in order to let it untangle itself in your brain.

It can help you work out the implications of various decisions, and in doing so narrow down the choices to a manageable set.

Guessing has another, almost magical property. It helps break the "I don't know what to do" panic that can start to set in when you're faced by a daunting or difficult task. If a problem makes your head ache, then it's best just to get going. The experience you gain while making essentially random decisions tends to make the entire task seem more bearable, and with enough guesses you're likely to stumble on something that is actually correct.

Remember, there's nothing wrong with being wrong – it's probably the fastest way to learn. If you fall off your bike, you'll try hard not to repeat the same mistake!

THE GOOD-ENOUGH SOLUTION

In many puzzles, we take as given that there's a single valid result, so we target our logic at finding that specific answer. However, in less well-defined situations we sometimes need to accept that a good-enough solution is sufficient. In many everyday situations, such as finding the quickest route by which to visit a list of locations, taking time to work out the perfect plan is not feasible – perhaps all you require is a *reasonable* solution. Even if you start with a relatively poor idea, simply making a start will give you the experience and information you need to refine this idea to a better one.

THE CHALLENGES OF LIFE

We learn all the time, not just when we read a book, solve a puzzle or watch a documentary. Our day-to-day activities form the cornerstone of mental fitness. We can exercise our minds by actively seeking out new ideas and experiences.

THE BENEFIT OF EXPERIENCE

You can find ways to stretch your brain every day. As an easy start, pick one small part of your daily routine and try doing it a different way in order to make you think about it afresh.

For example, you might take a new route to work or buy a different newspaper – find something to break your usual mould. Encourage yourself to think outside your normal comfort zone, and you'll be connecting up your brain for new types of retrieval and innovative thinking.

The more you explore the world, the wider your perspective, and the more ideas you'll have available to you. Travel, watch foreign films, and try to read a broad cross-section of news – not just current affairs, but also science and technology, new historical discoveries, and

"A man, though wise, should never be ashamed of learning more ..."

Sophocles (*c.*496–406BC)

more. Let other people's ideas feed your own.

Visit an art gallery and examine how different painters used subjects, shapes, colours or even textures to express their views of the world. Study old buildings in your street or town. Consider a piece of equipment that you use every day, such as your phone, and ask yourself how it works. Try mixing with people outside your usual circle of friends, family and colleagues.

BOOSTING YOUR CONFIDENCE

The mental habits that you develop from doing puzzles can actually be applied to life in general, improving your confidence and making you more capable of getting things done.

- Don't waste time regretting mistakes. If they're in the past, learn from them and move on. If they were things you *didn't* do, perhaps the lesson is to risk the unknown more often in future.

- Try to avoid making decisions based on habit or assumptions – think first, not afterwards.

- Look for alternative perspectives on a problem. For example, imagine how you'd find the worst rather than the best solution.

- When tackling weighty stuff, give your brain a chance of success – take a break with something simpler, such as an easy puzzle.

DOING IT EVERY DAY

You might be almost at the end of this book, but this is only the start of your work. Keeping your brain fit is a life-long quest. Try applying the tips given here so you continually expose your brain to novelty. Test yourself with puzzle magazines, and commit to reading new books regularly. And keep on thinking – challenge everything you see!

6
TOUGH
CHALLENGES

These knotty problems will really stretch your mental agility and stamina, and you might need more than one go at them, but they may well be the most satisfying puzzles of all once completed.

Many of the skills that you'll be using will have obvious practical applications in puzzles such as crosswords. They can also be highly beneficial in everyday life – for example, the verbal and logic skills may help you to prepare an outstanding presentation at work, or add to your enjoyment when reading classic literature.

Finally, once you've worked your way through the whole book, you may find it helpful to revisit any or all of the puzzles at intervals, to keep your skills sharp.

VERBAL TASKS 3

CRYPTIC THOUGHTS *(solutions on page 145)*

Can you solve the following cryptic crossword clues? The number of letters in each answer is given in brackets.

1 Took trap back for component (4)
2 Broken sword is made of letters (5)
3 Trains I left with legal guardian – you can see right through (11)
4 Fit tea initially inside being for something appropriate (9)

ATE MELON, LEMON TEA *(solutions on page 145)*

Can you join all of these words together into pairs? Each pair consists of words that are anagrams of each other.

Warbling	Recitals	Brigades	Resource
Caterers	Drainage	Indulged	Abridges
Retinues	Heartier	Rockiest	Sedative
Grannies	Earnings	Teenager	Enlisted
Deviates	Praising	Reunites	Earthier
Stricter	Deluding	Brawling	Gardenia
Listened	Stockier	Articles	Critters
Retraces	Generate	Recourse	Aspiring

CODE BREAKER *(solution on page 146)*

This grid is like a crossword, but the letters of the alphabet have been replaced by the numbers 1–26. Crack the code to solve the puzzle.

1	5	8	6	22	1		24	26	17	8	4	11
16			18		6		14					7
4		4	15	7	8	25	6	12	24	13		6
24		7		9		6		7		14		4
12	24	13	21	9	24	1	15		6	26	14	26
19		14		24		1		16		22		1
	6	3	14	26	11		2	14	4	8	25	
4		26		3		7		1		13		6
7	25	24	4		7	20	15	24	23	24	12	1
26		1		6		24		12		10		9
7		7	20	13	7	1	1	24	10	7		7
3				25		12		14				7
7	22	24	12	7	22		24	26	1	12	7	16

A B C D E F G H I J K L M N O P Q R S T U V W X Y Z

1	2	3	4	5	6	7	8	9	10	11	12	13
										Y		

14	15	16	17	18	19	20	21	22	23	24	25	26
									B	I		

FAMILY STORY *(solutions on page 146)*

This grid contains six triplets of related words. Can you draw lines to link each group of three synonyms?

Straightening	Tending	Transporting
Nursing	Obfuscate	Stirring
Moving	Scenting	Conceal
Smelling	Shifting	Ordering
Tidying	Touching	Sniffing
Obscure	Caring	Relocating

TWIN TROUBLE *(solutions on page 146)*

By selecting a single letter from each pair of letters here, can you work out which word is written on each line?

1 OE OE RE IE UE
2 GH HI AE ST EU ST
3 DE EI OE ER EA ME EA
4 LR AR LR GL AE ST ST EY
5 EA MN EA EA RL OU BD IE CM

ENCODED WISDOM *(solution on page 147)*

This quote has been encoded by replacing every letter with one a fixed number of places further forward or back in the alphabet; after Z, you continue with A. Can you work out the key and decode the quote?

Bwn wjz wswu pda xaop lneva pdwp heba dwo pk kbban eo pda ydwjya pk skng dwnz wp skng sknpd zkejc

Pdakzkna Nkkoarahp

FROM A TO Z *(solution on page 147)*

Place each of the letters A to Z once only into the empty squares of this grid so that each run of white squares spells out an English word.

A B C D E F G H I J K L M N O P Q R S T U V W X Y Z

VISUAL AND SPATIAL TASKS 3

TRI(T)ANGLE *(solution on page 147)*

How many triangles,
of all shapes and sizes,
can you count in
this picture?

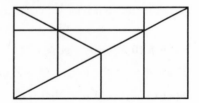

MATCH MAKER *(solutions on pages 147–8)*

14 matchsticks are laid out on a table, arranged so as to
make the following incorrect sum:

See if you can move or remove matches as directed in
the instructions below, using no trickery – just normal
numbers and basic maths. Reset the matches between
tasks. When moving them, you may not overlap any
further matches with one another.

1 Remove 3 matches to make a valid sum.
2 Remove 2 matches and move 1 match to make
a valid sum.
3 Remove 2 matches to make a valid sum.
4 Remove 1 match and move 1 match to make
a valid sum.
5 Move 2 matches to make a valid sum.

UPON REFLECTION *(solution on page 148)*

Study the image on the left. Can you draw it in the grid on the right, so it is reflected in the vertical "mirror line"?

A DIFFERENT ANGLE *(solution on page 148)*

Try to draw this picture rotated anticlockwise a quarter turn (90º).

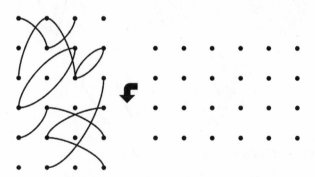

ZOOMED AROUND *(solutions on page 148)*

Five sections of this picture have been cut out, zoomed in, and then rotated by different amounts. Can you work out where each of the extracts below is taken from?

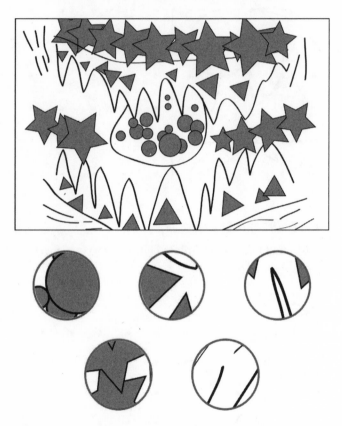

BOLDER FOLDER *(solution on page 149)*

If you were to cut out this shape and fold it along the straight lines, which of the three following cubes would result?

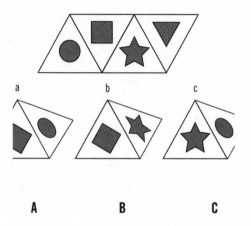

DIVIDE AND CONQUER *(solution on page 149)*

By drawing exactly three straight lines, can you subdivide this rectangle into four separate areas so that each area has precisely one of each shape? The lines can touch but must not cross each other.

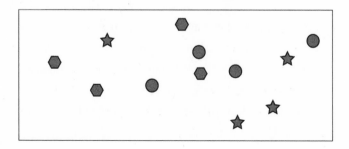

NUMERICAL TASKS 3

GREETING CARDS *(solutions on pages 149–50)*

You are given an ordinary deck of 52 playing cards, consisting of 4 suits of cards. Each suit contains A, 2, 3, 4, 5, 6, 7, 8, 9, 10, J, Q, K. You shuffle and deal 6 cards face up:

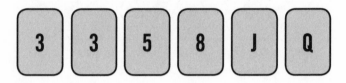

1 If you deal another card, what is the likelihood of it being a 3?

2 What is the probability of dealing a seventh card and finding that it is a J, Q or K? Is this more or less likely than the probability of dealing a 3, 4 or 5?

Now consider a situation where you have the six cards above already on the table, and are given a new set of 13 cards that contains one of each value. In sequence, they are A, 2, 3, 4, 5, 6, 7, 8, 9, 10, J, Q, K.

3 If you pick two cards at random from this new set of 13, what is the probability of being able to combine them with some of the six above to make a sequence of five cards, such as A, 2, 3, 4, 5?

4 More generally, if picking two random cards from this set of 13, what is the likelihood of combining them

with the six cards above to make a sequence of *either* four or five consecutive cards?

I NEED SUM HELP *(solutions on page 150)*

In the following sets of equations, each letter represents a whole number from 1 to 9. (The numbers are different for each set.) Can you work out which letter equals which number and solve the equations?

1 $3a + b = 9$ $b = 1 + a$

2 $ab = 40$ $a > b$

3 $ab = 20$ $bc = 30$

4 $2a + b = 7$ $ab = 3$

SQUARING UP *(solution on page 150)*

Place each of the numbers 1 to 9 into the nine empty squares in this grid so that the sums reading across and down are all correct. You may use each number once only.

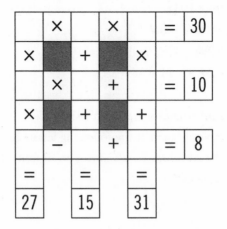

SEQUENTIALLY SPEAKING *(solutions on pages 150–51)*

Can you work out which number comes next in each of these mathematical sequences?

1	3	7	13	21	31	___
99	88	78	69	61	54	___
2	3	5	8	13	21	___
1	2	2	4	8	32	___
34	45	56	67	78	89	___

HURRY UP *(solutions on page 151)*

Use your estimation skills to get as close to the requested values as possible. Later on you can check against the solutions and see how you did! (Or use a calculator …)

1 45% of 9,975
2 A third of 747,747
3 17% of 61,234
4 $101 \times 98 \times 104$
5 $890 + 1120 - 570 + 445$
6 $35 \times (1,994 + 1,997 - 1,996)$
7 $9 \times 8 \times 7 \times 6 \times 11 \times 12 \times 13 \times 2$

COUNTING UP *(solutions on pages 151–2)*

Can you quantify each of the following letters or numbers? Some of the additions involved can be simplified, so look out for shortcuts!

1 How many multiples of 3 are there in the range 20–50?

2 How many prime numbers are there that are less than 50?

3 How many multiples of either 3 or 9 are there less than 100?

4 How many times does the letter "a" appear when you write out the numbers less than 100 in words?

5 And how many "e"s are there in the numbers less than 100?

CROSS SUMS *(solution on page 152)*

Give this Kakuro puzzle a try. Place a digit from 1 to 9 into every square so that each horizontal or vertical run of consecutive white squares adds up to the clue given at the left or the top of the run. No number can be repeated in the solution to any individual clue.

LOGIC AND REASONING TASKS 3

SUDOKU EXTRA AREAS *(solution on page 152)*

This Sudoku puzzle has an extra feature, which provides more clues. Can you not only place each of the digits 1 to 9 into each row, column, and bold-lined 3 × 3 box, but also place 1 to 9 into each of the four shaded 3 × 3 boxes? (It may help to make small notes in pencil, in the corners of the squares, to guide you as you work.)

2	9						6	3
6			3		1			7
	7			9			5	
	3			6			4	
4			2		3			9
1	5						7	6

FINGER MAZE *(solutions on page 153)*

Place your forefingers (or two pencils) on the two shapes marked with a +. Now try sliding each finger (or pencil) in turn from one shaded shape to another, along a joining line marked with the symbol that the *other* one is currently on. Can you move both onto the same piece?

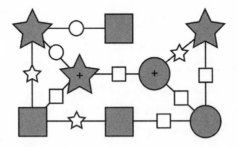

Once you've found one solution, find a second solution by which you finish with both fingers (or pencils) on a different piece.

ODD-ONE-OUT ROUND 3 *(solutions on page 153)*

Can you identify the odd word out in each set of five?

Primrose	Mate	Navy
Foxglove	Biography	Sky
Hyacinth	Graph	Cerulean
Daisy	Leaf	Daisy
Rosemary	Mobile	Cobalt

FORGOTTEN TREASURE *(solution on page 153)*

Some recent guests at the Welcome Hotel were very forgetful when checking out, and left certain items behind. Can you work out which hotel staff member found which item, left by which guest, and where in the guest's room the item was found?

Staff members: Dave Thane; Charles Berry; Sue Moss; Ruth Jones; Valerie Crawford
Items found: diamond necklace; love letters; Oscar statuette; polkadot suitcase; $10,000 cash
Guests: Jane Bond; Steve Harrod; Julie Katz; Katherine Arnold; Peter Downing
Where: behind the curtains; by the basin; hotel brochure; room service menu; under a pillow.

- The item found by Dave was not left by the woman who checked in as Jane Bond.
- Valerie found the Oscar statuette but it wasn't beneath a pillow or behind curtains.
- The room-service menu concealed a set of love letters.
- It wasn't Charles who found Steve Harrod's hotel brochure stuffed with cash.
- Katherine Arnold's diamond necklace wasn't found by Dave or Ruth, and neither did they find the $10,000 cash.
- The man who accidentally left something behind the curtains didn't have it found by Dave.

Here's another Slitherlink puzzle for you to try.
It can be solved purely by logic, and just like every
other puzzle here there is only one solution. See pages
86–7 for a reminder of the instructions and an example.

```
  0    2    2    2    3    2
3      2 1      3 1    1 1
  2    1 1    1    0    3
2    1    1    1    2    0
2    2    3    3 2    2 3
2 1      2    2    3    2
    2    3    3    1    3
3 1 2    1    1 2    2 3 1
2 1 2    1 1    3    1 2 2
  2    2    3    1    2
  1    2    2    3      2 2
  3 3    1 3    2    3    2
  2    1    2    3    2    2
  2    1    3    1 2    2
2 1    0 1      3 2        1
2    3    2    2    3    0
```

MEMORY TASKS 3
NUMBER GRID

Study the following grid of numbers for two minutes, then cover it and write as many of the numbers as possible in the empty grid beneath.

3	12	13	19	8
11	1	6	4	18
17	16	2	14	20
10	5	7	15	9

WORD LIST

Study this grid of words for up to two minutes, then cover it and write as many words as you can remember in the empty grid below.

Duck	Tree	Blender	Mechanism	Purple
Treacle	Spoon	Television	Piano	Night
Tracker	Cereal	Doughnut	Monkey	Planet

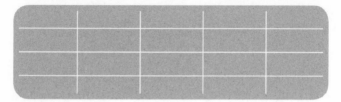

CAN YOU FACE IT?

Look at this list of faces for as long as you feel you need, then cover it and try to draw the same group of faces in the empty circles below.

THE ORDERING OF THE WORDS *(solutions on page 154)*

Below are two jumbled sentences. Study each one in turn, then cover it. Try to recall it, using the italic words as a guide.

is place stay wish a never in. we to but go a to Solitude wish to

a a but go in. is never place Solitude stay to to to we wish wish

the of hallmark the journalist The is misuse statistics. of modern

hallmark is journalist misuse modern of of statistics. the the The

Now cover all of the above and try un-jumbling both sentences in your head.

SENTENCED TO MEMORY

Study these four nonsensical sentences for two minutes, then cover them and attempt to recall each one verbatim. The first word of each sentence is given as a reminder.

- Interrogation is a subjugation of the imagination of the nation
- Transparency is translucency writ large by profligate light
- Indispensable dreams flitter thoughts through filtered times
- This great dispensary of the years lies buried in tatters

- Interrogation ...
- Indispensable ...
- Transparency ...
- This ...

VISUALIZE THIS (TWICE)

Study this pattern for as long as you need, then cover it. Try to reproduce the straight lines only, then repeat with the curved lines.

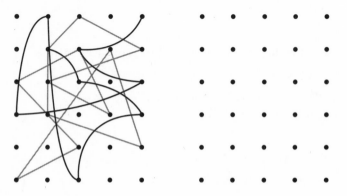

SOLUTIONS: VERBAL

Cryptic thoughts

1 **PART**: "Took trap back" indicates that "trap" should be written backwards, giving "PART" – a component.

2 **WORDS**: "Broken" is a hint that "sword" is to be broken up, giving "WORDS". "Is made of letters" is a straight clue for "words".

3 **TRANSPARENT**: "Trains I left" indicates that the first part is "Trains" after "I left" – ie after "I" is removed, giving "TRANS". "With" indicates that this should be joined to a "legal guardian": a PARENT. The result is something "you can see right through".

4 **BEFITTING**: "Tea initially" indicates the first letter of "tea", or "T". "Fit tea initially inside being" tells us to place "fit" and "T" inside "being". This makes "BeFITTing", which indeed is "appropriate".

Ate melon, lemon tea

Indulged & Deluding	Earnings & Grannies
Recourse & Resource	Abridges & Brigades
Reunites & Retinues	Brawling & Warbling
Stricter & Critters	Enlisted & Listened
Articles & Recitals	Teenager & Generate
Sedative & Deviates	Earthier & Heartier
Caterers & Retraces	Gardenia & Drainage
Stockier & Rockiest	Aspiring & Praising

Code breaker

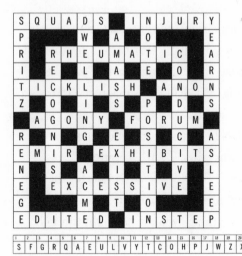

Family story

Straightening, Tidying, Ordering

Nursing, Tending, Caring

Transporting, Relocating, Shifting

Obfuscate, Obscure, Conceal

Stirring, Touching, Moving

Scenting, Sniffing, Smelling

Twin trouble

1 EERIE

2 HIATUS

3 DIORAMA

4 LARGESSE

5 ANAEROBIC

Encoded wisdom

To decrypt the message, shift each letter 4 places later in the alphabet – so, for example, A becomes E.

Far and away the best prize that life has to offer is the chance to work hard at work worth doing.

Theodore Roosevelt

From A to Z

SOLUTIONS: VISUAL AND SPATIAL

Tri(t)angle

There are 12 triangles.

Match maker

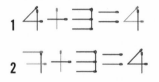

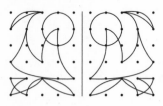

Upon reflection

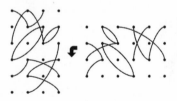

A different angle

Zoomed around

Bolder folder

The solution is cube A.

Divide and conquer

You can solve this by placing small line fragments where you know part of a line must go, such as between two identical shapes. Then it's fairly straightforward to join these up into the solution:

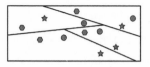

SOLUTIONS: NUMERICAL
Greeting cards

1 There are 2 left in the 46 cards that remain in the deck, so the probability is 2/46, or 1/23.

2 There are 10 J, Q or K cards left in the deck of 46, so the likelihood of one of these is 10/46 or 5/23. There are 9 of the 3, 4, 5 cards, for a 9/46 likelihood. Therefore J, Q, K is more likely.

3 You need a 9 and a 10 to get 8, 9, 10, J, Q. The likelihood of the first card being either a 9 or a 10 is 2 in 13; the likelihood of the second being the other one of the pair is then 1 in 12. Together the probability is 2 in 13 times 1 in 12, or 2/(12 × 13) = 2/156 = 1/78.

4 You can pick any of these pairs: 2 & 4, 4 & 6, 6 & 7, 9 & 10, 10 & K. The likelihood of any one of these is

1/78, so the overall probability is the chance of any of these 5 events happening, or 5/78.

I need sum help

1 You can solve this by substituting one equation into the other. This gives a = 2, b = 3.

2 The only solution to ab = 40 is 5 × 8, so once we know a > b it must be a = 8, b = 5.

3 The solution to ab = 20 must be 5 × 4, and that to bc = 30 must be 5 × 6. The b and the 5 are in common between the two, so b = 5 and therefore a = 4 and c = 6.

4 You can solve this using substitution and the quadratic equation, but it's much easier to note that if ab = 3, then a and b are 1 and 3. For 2a + b = 7 to be true, we must have a = 3 and b = 1.

Squaring up

1	×	5	×	6	=	30
×		+		×		
3	×	2	+	4	=	10
×		+		+		
9	−	8	+	7	=	8
=		=		=		
27		15		31		

Sequentially speaking

43: the difference increases by 2 each time.

48: the difference decreases by 1 each time.

34: each number is the sum of the previous two.

256: each number is the product of the previous two.

100: each number is 11 greater than the previous one.

Hurry up

1 About 4,500 (4,488.75 precisely).

2 About 250,000 (249,249 precisely).

3 About 10,000: 17% is roughly 1/6 of 100% (10,205 2/3 precisely).

4 About 1,000,000: each number is roughly 100 (1,029,392 precisely).

5 About 2,000 (1,885 precisely).

6 About 70,000 – the numbers in brackets are about 2,000 + 2,000 – 2,000, or 2,000 (69,825 precisely).

7 About 10,000,000 – round each number to the nearest 10 and ignore the 2 (10,378,368 precisely).

Counting up

1 **10 multiples**: 21 (7 × 3) up to 48 (16 × 3), so 10 multiples in all.

2 **15 primes**: 2, 3, 5, 7, 11, 13, 17, 19, 23, 29, 31, 37, 41, 43, 47.

3 **33 multiples**: we can ignore the multiples of 9, since they are all multiples of 3. They start at 3 (1 × 3) and run up to 99 (33 × 3).

4 **0 times**: the first number with an "a" in is (arguably) "a hundred", or perhaps "hundred and one", or "one thousand".

5 **146 times**: you can count "one" to "nine" – "e" occurs eight times. "Ten" to "nineteen" – 24 times. Then "twenty", "seventy", "eighty", and "ninety" each have one or two "e"s in the 10 numbers that start with them, so that's 5 × 10 = 50 times. "One" to "nine" occur another eight times as suffixes in the form "twenty-something" to "ninety-something", giving another 8 × 8 = 64. In total, 8 + 24 + 50 + 64 = 146.

Cross sums

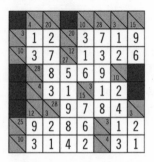

SOLUTIONS: LOGIC AND REASONING

Sudoku extra areas

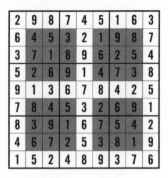

Finger maze

Label each shape from "a" to "h", starting at the top left and working left to right and top to bottom. The two shortest routes are as follows:

de ae ac fc gc gh gg

and

de ae ac fc fh ef df ff

Odd-one-out round 3

Foxglove: all the rest can be used as girls' names.

Leaf: all the rest form common words when prefixed with "auto".

Daisy: all the rest are shades of blue.

Forgotten treasure

Ruth   Suitcase   Peter Downing   Behind the curtains
Charles   Diamond necklace   Katherine Arnold
Under a pillow
Valerie   Oscar statuette   Jane Bond   By the basin
Dave   Love letters   Julie Katz   Room service menu
Sue $10,000 cash   Steve Harrod   Hotel brochure

Slither-think

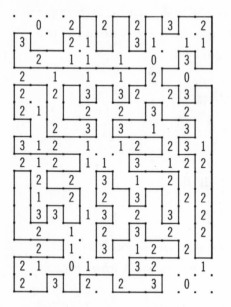

SOLUTIONS: MEMORY TASKS

The ordering of the words

The two most likely un-jumbled sentences are:

Solitude is a place we wish to go to but never wish to stay in.

The hallmark of the modern journalist is the misuse of statistics.

FURTHER READING

This selection includes books that provide more information on the brain and those that offer tips to help you build on particular mental skills.

Bracey, Ron *Boost your IQ: Tips and Techniques for a Sharper Mind*, Watkins 2018

Bridger, Darren and David Lewis *Think Smart, Act Smart: How to Make Decisions and Achieve Extraordinary Results*, Watkins 2018

Eastaway, Rob *Any Ideas? Tips and Techniques to Help you Think Creatively*, Watkins 2017

Hale-Evans, Ron *Mind Performance Hacks: Tips & Tools for Overclocking Your Brain*, O'Reilly 2006

Jeffrey, Andrew *Mastering Numbers: Everyday Mathematics Made Simple*, Watkins 2018

MacDonald, Matthew *Your Brain: The Missing Manual*, O'Reilly 2008

Moore, Gareth *The Mammoth Book of Brain Games*, Robinson 2014

O'Shea, Michael *The Brain: A Very Short Introduction*, Oxford University Press 2005

Stafford, Tom and Matt Webb *Mind Hacks: Tips & Tricks for Using Your Brain*, O'Reilly 2004

Tipper, Michael *Instant Recall: Tips And Techniques To Master Your Memory*, Watkins 2018

AUTHOR'S WEBSITE

For daily brain-training exercises from Dr Gareth Moore, please visit www.BrainedUp.com.

AUTHOR'S ACKNOWLEDGMENTS

Many thanks to my family for years of proof-solving puzzles of all types and varieties. You're a living testament to the power of keeping your brain fit! Thanks also to everyone at Duncan Baird, whose hard work and amazing attention to detail helped make this book what it is.